JOY IN THE DESERT

50 YEARS

OF GOSPEL BLESSING IN

BOTSWANA

JOY IN THE DESERT

50 YEARS
OF GOSPEL BLESSING IN
BOTSWANA

Clark Logan

RITCHIE

John Ritchie Publishing
40 Beansburn, Kilmarnock, Scotland

ISBN-13: 978 1 914273 03 2

Copyright © 2021 by John Ritchie Ltd.
40 Beansburn, Kilmarnock, Scotland

www.ritchiechristianmedia.co.uk

All Bible quotations are taken from the Authorised (King James) Version.

Kalahari Sunset

(Cover design by Brian Chalmers Design Services)

Typeset by John Ritchie Ltd., Kilmarnock
Printed by Bell & Bain Ltd., Glasgow

For all the friends who have prayed
and continue to pray
for Botswana

Sekaka se tlaa itumela

The desert shall rejoice (*Isaiah 35.1*)

CONTENTS

LIST OF ILLUSTRATIONS

FOREWORD

Joy in the Desert is a record of what God has done in Botswana over the past fifty years through a small band of devoted Christian workers. It is by no means a complete record – a great deal more will be revealed and rewarded at the judgment seat of Christ.

Those who responded to the Lord's call to serve Him in Botswana left the comforts of home and the security of successful careers. With no guaranteed salary and no sponsoring body supporting them, they went in faith, trusting God to meet their every need. He never once let them down! Their object in going was to preach and teach the message of the Bible and to establish local churches according to the principles outlined in the New Testament.

They did this, and for over fifty years God has richly blessed their service. It must be acknowledged that in doing so they have also significantly contributed to the material and medical welfare of many among whom they worked, all 'free of charge'. They have sought to show out as well as tell out the love of Christ.

This record of their work is firmly set within the context of life in Botswana. You will learn of the country's topography, history, culture and customs, and how these all combine to impact the work of spreading the gospel. Furthermore, you will be challenged and humbled as you read of the devotion of these men and women as they faithfully served their Master and the people to whom He has sent them, often in trying circumstances. Lastly, your heart and voice will rise in joyful praise of Him who "is able to do exceeding abundantly above all that we ask or think".

For twenty-two years it was my privilege to receive regular updates of the work and progress of these noble Christian workers. For me, it is a great joy to see some of that material and so much more brought together and presented in this permanent form.

I heartily recommend to you *Joy in the Desert*. I am sure that all who read it will be abundantly blessed and encouraged in their service for the best of masters, our Lord Jesus Christ.

Willie Houston
Kilmarnock
Scotland
April 2021

INTRODUCTION

Botswana has a unique charm that many of us love: the warmth of the people, the sight of a glorious sunset, the sound of children singing, the smell of the first rain upon the parched earth, and the taste of a steaming bowl of sour porridge on a crisp winter's morning.

This volume aims to tell the true story of how the lives of men and women, and boys and girls, in Botswana have been transformed by the power of the gospel of Christ. It has been our joy to witness God's blessing over many years in this desert land, and it has been an honour to serve Him here.

Memories fade quickly, but even if we had perfect recall, this brief record must be regarded as incomplete. While we may readily tell of what men and women have done, none of us can discern the full picture of what God has done or is doing. He often works behind the scenes. Then again, God will continue to work, long after our labours are over. This volume represents a partial record at a point in time, but the full story awaits a future day of heavenly review.

The men and women whose service for the Lord is described within these pages have one thing in common: they have taken the Word of God to be their only guide. For just over 50 years they have worked unitedly, seeking to follow the practice of the early Christians, even in these challenging times. They share the conviction that the first-century principles of the early church still work today.

I hope that this record will gladden your heart and cause you to praise God, giving thanks for what He has done. I also hope that through these pages you will enjoy meeting some of our friends in Botswana – trophies of grace! Perhaps it will encourage you to carrying the good news of the gospel to your own family, friends, and neighbours, just where you are, or even to others farther afield.

I wish to thank three friends: Bert Cargill of St Monans, Willie Houston of Kilmarnock, and Letsibogo Molebatsi of Gaborone who gave generously of their time and expertise to read through the complete manuscript and make valuable suggestions. Bert and his wife, Isobel, have faithfully supported the work in Botswana, prayerfully and practically, for many years and refreshed us with their personal visits. Willie Houston, the former secretary of the Lord's Work Trust based in Kilmarnock, kindly agreed to write the Foreword. He too has sought to encourage the Lord's work and workers all over the world. Letsibogo is a respected elder in the Gaborone assembly and a close and longstanding friend.

My thanks are also due to the family and friends of Jim and Irene Legge, the staff of Echoes International, as well as missionary colleagues and local believers who have provided recollections, old reports, photographs and more recent news about the gospel work in this country. The Endnotes acknowledge permission to use excerpts from previously published material. As always, the friends at 'Ritchie's' were companions on the journey and eased the winding pathway to publication.

Clark Logan
Tlokweng
Botswana
April 2021

Chapter 1

THE LAND AND THE PEOPLE

The Land

Arriving at Sir Seretse Khama airport from overseas on a summer's afternoon can literally take a first-time visitor's breath away. On descending the steps from the aircraft, a wave of heat rises to meet you; it is best compared to opening an oven door. The well-packed shoulder bag can suddenly seem heavier, and the jacket that was perfectly appropriate for a winter's day overseas, now feels like an encumbrance. By the time you complete the short walk to the terminal building, you will be perspiring!

Another significant factor, not immediately apparent, is the altitude. Much of Botswana is situated at about 4,000 feet above sea level. Anyone suffering from a cardiac or respiratory problem may feel minor discomfort at first. Even when we return to our adopted homeland from a visit overseas, we can take a few days to acclimatise again. Despite its elevation, most of the country appears flat and there are no mountain ranges. The highest feature is Monalanong Hill, near Otse in the south-east, at an elevation of 4,902 feet (1,494 metres) above sea level.

These factors are reminders that Botswana is a large, landlocked desert country situated on an elevated plain in the centre of southern Africa. We are surrounded by Namibia to the west, Angola and Zambia to the north, Zimbabwe to the east, and South Africa to the south. The beautiful beaches and refreshing ocean breezes of Cape Town are 1,000 miles to the south. The sand of the Kalahari Desert covers over 70 per cent of the country and, therefore, the central landmass is sparsely populated. The total population of the country in 2020 was just over 2.35 million people. The majority of the residents are found living in the two cities and larger towns and villages on the eastern side. Around the periphery are several other towns or large villages.

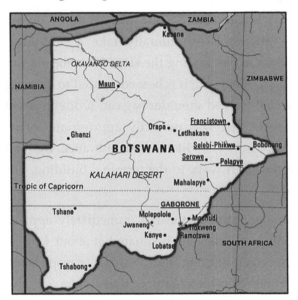

Map of Botswana
(Locations of the six assemblies are underlined)

Being a desert land, we have known extended periods of severe drought, notably in the 1980s when there were seven consecutive years of scant rainfall. More recently, in 2017, conditions were so extreme that the water level in the Gaborone Dam fell to 1.7 per cent – basically only mud remained! A national emergency was declared. Shops ran out of bottled water and hardware stores had a major run in sales of water pumps and reservoir tanks as people belatedly tried to prepare for long-term restrictions.

There are only a few perennial rivers. However, paradoxically, when the seasonal rains do come, they can be torrential and cause sudden flooding. This occurred in 2000 when the Gaborone Dam overflowed and our home village of Tlokweng was cut off from the capital for several days. The two connecting road bridges were submerged. While it is no surprise that Botswana does not have a navy, the Botswana Defence Force does have its own scuba-diving team. They are sometimes called upon to search for and recover the bodies of those who have drowned in the floods.

The Kalahari Desert is mostly semi-arid: scrub bush covers a large proportion of it although there are stretches of barren sand dunes. On account of the altitude and distance from the sea, temperatures can be extreme. In the mid-summer month of January, temperatures can reach 44 degrees Celsius (111 degrees Fahrenheit). Early one summer's morning, we discovered our pickup truck had a shattered windscreen. It was not the work of thieves as we first thought; a canister of compressed foam, normally kept in the glovebox, had exploded in the heat. The inside of the vehicle was peppered with sharp fragments of metal that could have caused serious injury to any passenger.

The climate can affect the routine of everyday life. One significant problem is that personal energy levels drop significantly after months of unrelenting summer heat. The coolness of the early morning makes it the best time to get things done. The old hospital adage applies: 'An hour before nine o'clock is worth two hours afterwards.' We do occasionally catch ourselves dreaming of a beach walk and balmy ocean breezes.

The dry season months, April to September, present blue skies, pleasant daytime temperatures, and cool nights. In mid-winter, the temperature at night can drop to minus 15 degrees Celsius (seven degrees Fahrenheit), particularly in the central desert area. The month of June bears the name *Seetebosigo* which means 'Don't go out at night!' We sometimes have frost, but we have never seen snow. The cloudless, pollution-free winter skies are ideal for stargazing and admiring the constellations of the southern hemisphere such as Orion and Pleiades. The beauty of creation prompts us to praise our Creator who made them all (Job 9.9).

The Okavango Delta in north-west Botswana is world famous for its amazing wildlife. The word 'delta' usually refers to a coastal area where a river fans out into smaller tributaries as it meets the sea. In the case of the Okavango, it is an inland river fanning out like a triangle, but then dissipating in the sand of the desert. The headwaters of the river originate in the Angolan highlands and seasonally flood the delta. However, with more peaceful conditions in Angola, there is increased human development and water usage in the catchment area. The concern is that this could adversely affect water levels in the delta habitat.

Tourism is one of our country's largest revenue-earners. The preferred model has leaned towards the low-volume, high-cost approach to tourism. World leaders and international celebrities arrive by private jet to stay in exclusive camps in the most beautiful areas. They go on game drives or hunting expeditions during the day and then are wined and dined in luxury each evening. One of our acquaintances from Serowe days was a professional hunting-guide for such parties. On one year's tips alone, he financed the building of a new outdoor swimming pool at his home. Prince Charles would visit Botswana and meet up with his friend, the famous author, Sir Laurens van der Post. They would camp out in the bush and discuss Jungian philosophy, environmental issues and much else besides. Van der Post became a mentor in the Prince's life and was also chosen to be a godfather to Prince William.

Chobe Elephants

The Chobe River area in the north is renowned for its large herds of elephants and the other species that make up 'The Big Five' – rhino, buffalo, lion, and leopard. In 1975, the actress, Elizabeth Taylor, remarried Richard Burton in the Chobe Game Park. One day, on a safari, she felt unwell and was assisted at a small local clinic. She was so grateful that she offered to sell one of her diamond rings, then worth one million dollars, and give it to the Botswana government, but specifically for that bush clinic. The story goes that the government could not promise to spend such a large sum on one small remote clinic and the donation did not proceed.

The People

The indigenous people of the Kalahari are thought to have inhabited the central desert area for millennia. They are experts at coping with the harsh environment. Anthropologists and linguists talk of the San and the Khoe Bushmen. The San are hunter-gatherers, surviving on edible leaves, fruits and roots, but also hunting for game by tracking animals for many hours until they are able to kill their prey using poison-tipped arrows or spears. It is a mistake to think of them as one homogenous group and although the term Sesarwa is commonly used when speaking of the language of the bushmen, there are several different dialects within this grouping. Not many outsiders have mastered these languages with their unusual click sounds; it is an even more difficult task to commit them to writing. The Khoe people were also nomadic but more accustomed to herding livestock.

The question of the origins of the people of Botswana is much debated. There are no early written records, but it is thought that Bantu farmers moved down from central Africa and intermarried with the San and Khoe. From a group classified as Sotho-Tswana (c. AD 900), many branches developed resulting in numerous tribal groupings. Today in Botswana, eight major tribes are identified, but it is recognised that there are many other smaller tribes that make an important contribution to the modern nation.

Each tribe has a special animal symbol that is revered by that tribe, for example, the Bakwena tribe, as their name indicates, are the people of the crocodile. These are the people among whom David Livingstone lived. Their tribal capital is the village of Molepolole, some 37 miles west of Gaborone.

A tumultuous period of history began in the 1820s, known as the *Difaqane* ('crushing'). Larger tribal groupings began to threaten smaller ones in a quest for dominance and larger territory. Shaka, the Zulu king, and Mzilikazi of the Ndebele were famous warriors of that time. There was also the added complication of Boer expansionism beyond the Cape Colony. The next few decades were filled with turmoil and it would be some time before displaced Batswana returned to their original homelands. The introduction of firearms meant that European traders were kept busy selling guns to the various tribal chiefs who saw the acquisition of firearms as a way to secure their position. Another persistent factor that influenced resettlement was the presence of tsetse fly in certain areas. This insect transmitted disease which could be fatal to both cattle and humans.

The Batswana tribes reorganised their ruling structures and consolidated their territory. By the end of the 19th century, three chiefs – Khama III of the Bamangwato, Sebele I of the Bakwena, and Bathoen I of the Bangwaketse – made a famous visit to London, travelling with W. C. Willoughby, their translator. There, in 1895, they appealed to Queen Victoria for continued British protection in Bechuanaland. At that time, they feared the dominating influence of Cecil Rhodes. His commercial empire was fast expanding in line with his aspirations of controlling the 'Cape to Cairo' route. The chiefs won the day and British protection preserved their identity and territory. The administration of the territory continued peacefully, though some might describe it more as the 'benign neglect' of a colonial backwater. There was limited development due to the harsh climate and lack of resources. A sparsely populated desert land was never going to be a priority for an imperialist superpower. However, the 19th century was also the time when providentially the gospel was brought to the region by missionaries from overseas.

'The Three Chiefs' and Willoughby

In the Second World War (1939-45), Batswana soldiers fought on the British side. They were reported to be 'excellent workers, conscientious, and unusually strong'. Following the war, the marriage of Seretse Khama to an Englishwoman, Ruth Williams, on 29th September 1948, came as a challenge to traditional structures and national identity. The ripple effect was felt not only in London but also in Pretoria, the capital of apartheid South Africa. Seretse Khama was the heir to the throne of the large Bamangwato tribe. Seretse's uncle, who had been Regent for many years, and members of his own tribe were initially opposed to the marriage. An inter-racial marriage on South Africa's border was also going to cause disquiet in that country. The full story is one of intrigue but through it all Seretse and Ruth were unwavering in their support of one another. He would eventually be welcomed back to Botswana with his bride. He had renounced the chieftainship of the Bamangwato tribe as a precondition of his return, but the people still regarded him as their leader.

After independence in 1966, Seretse Khama became the first President of the new nation, riding a wave of overwhelming public support and winning the popular vote. The success of Seretse and Ruth's strong marriage had another positive effect: the people of Botswana are tolerant of different races. Many of us here are 'colour-blind' and accept other people just as they are. Our national flag is mainly blue, representing *pula* (rain). The black and white stripes represent the racial harmony that exists, and they also remind us of the zebra, our national animal.

The Modern Nation

Botswana is only one of many African countries that became independent in the 1960s. It gained independence from Britain in 1966 in a peaceful and diplomatic way. While becoming a member of the Commonwealth, it was still one of the 15 poorest countries in the world. It might have remained so but for the discovery of rich deposits of diamonds. A rapid course of nationwide development began, fueled by the new source of revenue. This continues until today, even though diamond sales have declined in more recent years. The world's second-biggest uncut diamond, after the Cullinan diamond, was discovered in Botswana in 2018. The 1,758-carat stone was larger than a tennis ball. Three years previously, another large diamond known as 'Lesedi La Rona' (Our Light) had been discovered and was sold for $53m (£41.1m).

The government of Botswana used the new wealth to build roads, schools and clinics. They also upgraded the country's infrastructure, particularly as regards supplying electricity, water and telecommunications to all areas of the country. Large urban housing developments began appearing, with nearby shopping malls and high-rise office blocks. Village life was also affected, albeit at a slower pace.

A Study in Contrasts - Rural and Urban Botswana

We moved to Gaborone in 1984 and found it to be a quiet little town. One could drive through it on the narrow roads with their rough verges in about ten minutes, at any time of night or day.

Now it can take an hour just to reach the city centre from the outskirts, on modern highways. There was much amusement when the first traffic lights were installed (known locally as 'robots'). Road junctions became play areas for children who would gather on one side of the road, press the button to watch the lights change, march over to the other side, promptly turn around and repeat the process. The street junctions were also littered with debris from the many accidents that were caused by drivers not knowing what to do when confronted with the multiple changing colours. The first escalator in a downtown store provided another opportunity for children to have fun.

On the political scene, the ruling Botswana Democratic Party has retained its dominance but there have been times when the opposition has gained more influence. The BDP's party symbol is the old-fashioned car jack; the idea being to lift the nation up. President Sir Seretse Khama was much loved and he set a pragmatic course for the nation, handling the tensions of being a front-line African state which was at the same time almost totally dependent upon apartheid South Africa for its access to ports and for the importation of consumer goods. When Seretse Khama died in 1980, Vice-President Masire took over. Sir Ketumile Masire ruled for 18 years and oversaw a period of rapid economic growth and prosperity. Again, he had to walk a fine line, particularly regarding the relationship with South Africa. However, Botswana still functioned as a 'front-line state' and offered sanctuary to political refugees.

Those of us who lived through the experience will never forget the night of 14 June 1985. South African commandos crossed over the border into Botswana to lead attacks against what they believed to be members of the *uMkhonto we Sizwe*, the military wing of the African National Congress (ANC). Ten separate sites in Gaborone were attacked simultaneously that night including a home just behind our own in the Broadhurst area of the city. We were awakened by the sound of gunfire and loud explosions. We heard later in news reports that the man they were looking for in our locality had escaped but a woman was fatally shot. In all, 13 people were killed including a six-year-old boy, a 71-year-old-man, and three women. President Masire called the raid 'an act of brutality and violence' and said it was 'particularly deplorable' because he had repeatedly assured Pretoria that he did not allow guerrillas to use Botswana as a springboard for attacks on South Africa. Obviously, he was not believed.

Today Botswana functions as a parliamentary democracy with national elections held every five years. It has remained an island of peace and stability in an otherwise troubled region. We have been blessed with leaders who, despite their differences, have passed on the torch to their successors. The excesses of demagoguery seen frequently in some other Africa states have so far been avoided. Great challenges face the government at present: slower economic growth, rising unemployment, difficulties in diversifying the economy, the scourges of AIDS and Covid-19, and recurrent drought, to name but a few.

Society has been changing rapidly here too and people struggle to come to terms with new realities. These changes affect the work of the gospel and the functioning of local assemblies of Christians. With increasing affluence and a more competitive work environment, people can easily lose sight of spiritual priorities and be overtaken by the pressures of 'the rat race'. A few examples will be cited. These are common to other countries, but in Botswana these changes have been compressed into a much shorter period. We have Christians in assembly fellowship with postgraduate degrees whose parents could not read or write.

In earlier years we would visit around the areas where we lived and speak to the people. Open access to the yard of a home compound meant that one could enter, politely greet the family living there, sit down on a chair that would quickly appear, and have a good chat with the residents. Nowadays, because of increased crime, people are building high walls around their properties. These are known locally as 'stop nonsense'! Add to that an electrified perimeter fence, a locked steel gate, and two Rottweilers, and the would-be caller finds his or her options are much more limited.

In general, people who are poorer are more willing to listen to the gospel. This has always been the case; it was the same in the time of the Lord Jesus (Mark 12.37). The better educated and more affluent are too busy with a multiplicity of time-consuming tasks. The work environment in Botswana has changed in the last few decades and people are working much longer hours. Some of our finest believers who as young Christians attended nearly every assembly meeting, are now at the office by 7.30 in the morning and arrive home exhausted late in the evening. There is only time to have a quick wash, eat, and collapse into bed. This is not by choice, or even to earn extra money from overtime. This is routinely what employers are expecting from their workers and often there is no overtime payment offered; the boss makes the rules as he or she sees fit.

Another factor is that conscientious workers are promoted and given even more responsibility. As we observe these intense pressures on our Christian brothers and sisters, we can only pray for them and encourage them to go on in the ways of Christ. There are no easy answers; the solution is not to advise them to change jobs. Vacancies are scarce and options are limited. Even university graduates now wait for many months before finding any job, much less a job of their choice.

The Christian is reassured to know that the Lord is never surprised by any change. While we may need to adapt, we can be sure that He will always guide us as to how we can live out our faith and honour Him in any circumstance. He abides faithful.

Chapter 2

LANGUAGE AND CULTURE

The Beauty of Setswana

'We will meet tomorrow at the cows' horns' (*Re tlaa kopana ka moso, ka dinaka tsa kgomo.*) But whatever does this mean? In our language it describes an early-morning rendezvous, at the time when one can just see the horns of the cattle appearing through the mist. It sounds more inviting, if somewhat less precise than saying, 'Let's meet at 6.00 a.m.'

The beauty of Setswana, originally a pastoral language, only becomes apparent as one develops a knowledge of it. This takes time, much time. Most of us who have tried to gain a degree of fluency would readily confess that we will always be learners. We are constantly hearing unfamiliar words and phrases, and immediately our ears prick up. We are also aware of our limitations, for example, when old men talk about their cattle, they have a specialised vocabulary that few outsiders can follow. Then there are occasions when a Setswana poet is called upon to recite spontaneously a poem in praise of an honoured guest. We listen with a sense of wonderment but also bewilderment at this 'deep' Setswana.

Setswana is a Bantu language that has developed from the Sotho / Tswana language group. The people who are said to have moved from central Africa to settle further south are collectively described as Bantu. (In the context of language studies, the word *'Bantu'*, meaning 'people', is not derogatory). Linguists have proposed that these related languages developed from a common root. This large group of languages includes those commonly spoken in southern Africa such as Zulu, Khosa, Venda, Sotho and Setswana.

These languages share a grammatical structure that uses noun classes, verbal moods, and various tones to distinguish meaning. While it might help if a would-be learner had already studied English grammar, a modern European language such as French, and perhaps an ancient language such as Latin, a complete mental reset is required to tackle African languages. They have an elegance and complexity of their own, demanding our respect.

The Complexity of Setswana

Setswana has 10 classes of nouns so that, taking into account the singular and plural of each class, there are 20 different ways to say 'of' in relation to a noun. And yet, when these classes of nouns with their prefixes are mastered, the various grammatical constructions and phrases flow in a harmonic way which is delightful to the ear. Linguists describe this grammatical structure as being 'concordial'. (It may be helpful to indicate now that one person from Botswana is known as a *Motswana* and two or more people are referred to as *Batswana*.)

The missionary must learn the language to the best of his or her ability. The primary goal is to communicate the message of the gospel effectively to the people of Botswana, both young and old. The only way to learn the language is to study it, spending hours of hard labour and facing frustration at nearly every stage. There may be a few gifted individuals who can 'pick up' conversational Setswana quickly through everyday interaction. However, the missionary has a wider goal: beyond being able to converse in the language, there is also the need to be able to read, write, and translate it.

Language learning is a humbling experience. Second-language learning is accomplished much easier by a child. Our own children have confirmed this: growing up in the country, their tones are perfect and indistinguishable from a Motswana's, whereas ours will always betray our origins. Children have fewer inhibitions; their single motivation is to communicate, even if imperfectly. Older people are more concerned about avoiding making mistakes and looking foolish. And yet we must keep reminding ourselves that the language is one of the keys to reaching an individual's mind, heart, and conscience.

All of us have an embarrassing story to tell. Our late colleague, Jim Legge, used to describe in a graphic manner how he once preached a whole sermon on the lost nose (*nko*) rather than the lost sheep (*nku*). I was caught out too when, after moving to Gaborone, I invited our neighbours to our home to hear the gospel. My mistake was to mix up the tones of two words that were otherwise identical. Instead of informing our neighbours that it was a public meeting and we had no secrets, they must have been relieved to learn that we had no hyenas!

The Challenge of Translation

If preaching in Setswana is challenging enough, then so too is preaching by interpretation. At first, visiting preachers can find it disconcerting: they have to stop and start throughout their message, breaking their flow, causing some to rename the method, 'preaching by interruption'. Those accustomed to using alliteration discover that these aides-memoire are completely lost in translation. There will also be readjustments necessary if the preacher favours quotations of hymns and poems. A good interpreter can succeed in conveying the meaning, but the rhythms and rhymes of the English words cannot be retained. In general, a Setswana translation uses more words than English.

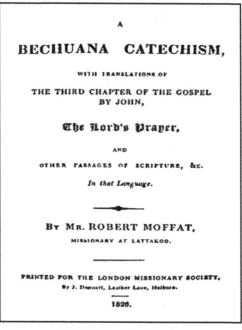

A

BECHUANA CATECHISM,

WITH TRANSLATIONS OF

THE THIRD CHAPTER OF THE GOSPEL
BY JOHN,

The Lord's Prayer,

AND

OTHER PASSAGES OF SCRIPTURE, &c.

In that Language.

By Mr. ROBERT MOFFAT,

MISSIONARY AT LATTAKOO.

PRINTED FOR THE LONDON MISSIONARY SOCIETY,
By J. Dennett, Leather Lane, Holborn.

1826.

Moffat's First Publication

On the positive side, preaching by interpretation gives the speaker time to think ahead and consider his next sentence. All the preacher needs to do is state a complete thought and a skilful interpreter can accurately express the true meaning. We are now blessed with men who know their own language well and are fluent in colloquial English. They also know their Bibles and are spiritually mature. They soon catch where the preacher is heading and what he is trying to convey to the audience. We sometimes tell visitors that 'If you take a coughing fit, don't worry. Your interpreter will be able to continue on his own and finish the message for you.'

Our Setswana Bible translation is based on the English Revised Version. It is a good if not a perfect translation, like many other translations. On occasions we might be tempted to inform the audience that the translation could be improved. This should be resisted at all costs for this reason: the current Setswana Bible is all that the Batswana have, particularly those who are not fluent in English. It is the Word of God to them. We should not undermine the integrity of this precious book.

There remain many difficulties and pitfalls. Nevertheless, if the language learner is burdened for his audience and motivated by love, the Lord can use even his or her feeblest efforts to be a blessing to the hearers.

A Changing Culture

The people of Botswana are gentle and peace-loving. They are also tolerant of others. The older generation is characterised by a respectful dignity – we call it 'botho'. Capturing the charm of our traditional ways has turned Alexander McCall Smith into a best-selling author. The exploits of the redoubtable Mma Ramotswe, a lady detective of unusual skill and insight, have charmed readers all over the world. Her love of a refreshing cup of redbush (rooibos) tea has also boosted the worldwide sales of this product by 70 per cent!

Like all cultures in our interconnected world, the culture of Botswana is changing rapidly. Exposure to international media, especially television and social media, means that a new fashion or fad that hits the streets of London or New York today, can be seen here tomorrow. The media do not only transmit the outward features of a lifestyle; they also influence values and attitudes. Traditional culture in all its aspects is under threat here as elsewhere. Our government has tried to preserve the basic elements of the national culture. Children at school are taught formal Setswana – most of them find the subject difficult – and time is set aside in the curriculum for traditional singing and dancing competitions. Virtues such as good manners and self-control are extolled.

Not many years ago, I was leaving the house when the lady who has helped Hazel in our home for over 30 years told me, 'RraSethunya (my African name), you can't go out dressed like that.' When I enquired why not, she told me, 'You are not wearing a belt. It is disrespectful.' I have long ago learnt the wisdom of stopping and listening to this lady. I immediately returned to the bedroom to make myself more presentable. It is a constant learning process that one ignores at his or her peril.

Politeness

According to traditional values here, a younger person is required to greet all elderly people in a mannerly way. In a family setting, dealing with a difficult matter requires a degree of finesse and diplomacy that is often lacking in western conversation. The Botswana way is to exchange full greetings and then one slowly broaches the relevant issue. This approach is less direct but more polite. One can learn so much by observing the skill and tact of others in these situations.

While there is great liberty and freedom of speech in Botswana, we have always been aware that it is wise to announce one's intentions regarding any proposed venture. Even back in those earlier days when our senior colleagues, Jim and Irene Legge, arrived in Serowe and began working there, they could not have said to themselves, 'We will go into the bush and start a clinic wherever we choose.' They had to work through the existing structures and health departments, fitting into the government's plans for the development of these services.

The same would apply to gospel preaching, for example, in the open-air. In a village, one cannot just set up wherever you choose, unannounced. The chief or headman of the area should be consulted, and his permission requested. This same principle holds good in towns and cities as well. There is rarely a refusal. The main requirement is to show respect for the institutions that have been in place for many generations.

Consultation

The traditional tribal structure throughout Botswana has centred on an outdoor meeting place known as the *kgotla*, usually identified by a palisade of wooden stakes and a flagpole flying the national flag near the centre of a village. This is where the chief still makes important public announcements and conducts extraordinary business. Nearby offices deal with everyday affairs. Larger villages are divided into areas with their own smaller kgotlas where a sub-chief or headman takes the lead. Visitors are advised to conduct themselves respectfully in this area of the village and refrain from taking photographs without permission.

While in the past the people of Botswana have not lacked brave warriors, their nature is not belligerent. They have a strong belief in the need to talk a matter through, relying upon negotiation rather than aggression. International disputes and crises in our region have been resolved successfully in this way. Even today, when there are issues of national importance, the President may tour various districts to explain his new policies at a kgotla meeting. Often the assembled local people have the liberty to raise matters of concern directly with the President. This arrangement is a unique feature of democracy in Botswana.

Cattle and Crops

Cattle have always been of vital importance to Batswana, even before the modern independent nation began exporting beef to the EEC (European Economic Community). Wealth is measured by the number of cattle a man possesses. However, it is rude to ask someone how many cattle they own, just as in other cultures one does not ask a person how much money they have in the bank.

Brahman Bull

The annual cycle of cultivation and herding determines the movements of rural populations. Most people have a village home but when the rains are due and the chief has sanctioned the ploughing, they will move out to the *masimo*, the fields, where they begin to plough and grow their crops (usually sorghum and maize but also melons, beans and other small vegetables). They have a simple dwelling there. A third dwelling may be found at the *moraka*, the cattle post, which can be found at another distant location. This constant migration is a significant factor in planning special meetings of believers or gospel outreaches. Overlook this fact of life and one can find that there are few people around to attend. The *malwapa*, home compounds, are deserted and the front gates are tied up with wire or locked.

Cultivation in Botswana using traditional methods is labour-intensive. The government assists farmers by providing seed for planting and tractors for ploughing but today it is a matter of concern that few young people are interested in cultivating the land. It is hard work. Clearing the ground then ploughing, sowing, weeding, guarding, reaping, threshing, bagging and storing the grain. There are numerous hurdles to be overcome – too little rain, too much sun, storms of wind and hail, infestation with parasites, plagues of rodents, locusts, and red-billed quelea. All of these factors militate against a good harvest. (There are many spiritual parallels.) Economics also plays a factor: inevitably, in a year with an abundant harvest the price of grain falls and the hard work yields less profit.

Weddings

We cannot leave the subject of cattle just yet. When it comes to weddings, cattle are all important because they are required for paying the bride price. Months of delicate negotiations precede the ceremony. The senior uncles from both families, representing the parents, meet together to agree on the details of the marriage, particularly the number of cattle that the man must pay. Once that payment is made in public, the couple is recognised in customary law as being married.

As far as Christian believers are concerned, most prefer that their marriage be solemnised 'in the presence of God' and in a place of worship. We advise our friends from the assembly fellowship to regard the day of the religious ceremony as the beginning of their marriage. We do this for the sake of their public testimony. Even if the bride price has already been paid, they should not live together but rather regard themselves as an engaged couple up until their wedding day. The young man and young woman and may also be pressurised by their unbelieving families to do as others do, by serving beer and playing loud music at their wedding. We are always encouraged to see them graciously but firmly take a stand.

The extended family is still important in Botswana and people are much more aware of their line of descendants than in many western societies. As for living relatives, they will be aware of their great uncles and aunts, second and third cousins, and other such distant connections. At wedding celebrations, the family elders from both sides begin by introducing themselves: 'I am .... the son of ... who was the son of ... who was the son of ... from the kgotla of ... in the village of ...'

Even though customs are changing, and young people mix more freely with one another, courtship is markedly different in Botswana. When a man approaches a lady for the first time and expresses an interest in her, it is interpreted as a serious matter that may progress to marriage. Many young people find it difficult to confide with their parents about such matters; often they come to us for advice. We try to give helpful counsel and guidance from the Bible before young believers marry.

A Christian Wedding

Funerals

Funerals are significant social gatherings in Botswana and often they are the best attended events. When someone dies, there are two perplexing questions that relatives might ask themselves: 'What did he die of?' Often this first question can be easily answered by a medical explanation such as, 'He died of heart failure.' However, there is an unspoken second question that can linger in some people's minds and trouble them: 'Who was responsible for his death?' The answer to this question is more problematic and involves a dark world of fear and suspicion. That is why it is common to have a detailed medical history read out at the funeral: a widow will want to make clear that she did everything possible to care for her sick husband. She was not responsible for his death. This underlying fear is another reason why people make strenuous efforts to attend a funeral: 'If I am not there, what might the family suspect?'

There are numerous funeral societies to which people pay a monthly subscription to have a fashionable send-off. Before a burial, relatives from afar begin arriving days before – they must be accommodated and fed several times each day. For up to a week there will be evening 'prayers' at the family home, just before sunset. Usually, all who attend receive a mug of tea and some bread after a short service. The Bible is read, and a message is given. When we are involved, we offer words of comfort if the deceased was a believer, but we always preach the gospel and present a challenge to the hearers.

As Christians, we are conscious of the need to be present to support our fellow believers. In their hour of sorrow, they can feel lonely and vulnerable, especially if the rest of the family do not share their faith. On occasion, relatives can be cruel and try to strip the widow of her meagre assets. The physical presence of true friends can ease these burdens.

Cooking at a Funeral

Apart from the basic requirements of printing an 'Order of Service', arranging a hearse etc., there is also a cultural obligation to feed all who attend on the day of the burial. Anyone can come; nobody will be turned away. A cow is killed, and porridge and beef are served. The men in particular look forward to *mokoto*, a large helping of beef fillet mixed with chopped-up intestines. The financial burden of a large funeral can literally bankrupt a family. Poorer families often receive government assistance 'in kind' – a tent for the mourners or maybe a simple coffin – and this is commendable.

In general, all cultures have distinctive features, some good and some bad. We must avoid the mistake of a blinkered superior view, as if western culture is the gold standard. It is not. There are features of western culture today that the world could well do without, and some of the positive aspects of African culture are worth emulating. In the fellowship of Christians, it is the love of Christ which reminds us constantly that we are one in Him. This love unites us. There is no expectation that someone from Ireland will become a real African, or vice versa, but in Christ, we share so much in common that other differences fade away. 'Them and us' becomes 'we together', bound up in the bundle of divine life.

Cultural awareness does not in any way change the truth of the gospel, but it does help those who preach the message to be more sensitive, more respectful and more understanding of the men and women to whom they speak. It also encourages us to be kind and supportive of one another. There was none so sympathetic as our Lord Jesus.

Chapter 3

OUR CHRISTIAN HERITAGE

The gospel reached the interior of southern Africa in the early 19th century. The explorer, Jan van Riebeeck, had arrived at the southern tip of the continent in 1652 under the auspices of the Dutch East India Company. He established a colony at the Cape of Good Hope so that passing Dutch trading ships could find anchorage and resupply there.

The majority of the early European settlers were linked with the Dutch Reformed Church although a smaller group of Germans were Lutheran in affiliation. A significant number of French Huguenots, fleeing Catholic persecution in Europe, were also assimilated into the Cape colony. The British assumed control and the administration of the area in 1806.

The subsequent years were shaped by tensions between the British and the Dutch, between these Europeans and the local African people, and between the African tribes themselves. Historians keep busy advancing theories to explain the reasons for these many conflicts. Few seem to acknowledge that human nature has not changed and the craving for power, control, territory and riches has corrupted every society since the Fall.

The Cape colony became the port of entry to the unexplored hinterland of southern Africa, not only for traders and adventurers but also for those bearing the message of the gospel. Five men will be mentioned covering two centuries of history. Four had strong ties to Scotland; the fifth was a converted African chief of great distinction. Their lives intertwined in providential ways.

Robert Moffat

Robert Moffat

This gospel pioneer was born in Ormiston, East Lothian, in 1795. After leaving school, Moffat was apprenticed as a gardener. He worked initially in Scotland and then later in Cheshire, England. When he left home, his mother made him promise that he would read the Bible every day. He lived to keep his word.

He was converted to Christ at the age of 17 and subsequently convicted as to missionary service when one evening, walking from High Leigh to Warrington, he saw a poster advertising a missionary meeting that had already taken place. Nevertheless, this stirred his interest and 'made him another man'.

He was 21 years of age when he set sail for southern Africa as a missionary recruit of the London Missionary Society. He arrived at Cape Town on 13th January 1817, and a year later made a trip to the north that resulted in his acquaintance with a feared and murderous renegade chief called Africaner. Moffat had been warned that the chief would kill him and use his skull for a drinking cup! What did happen was that after some months the chief was converted and lived to prove the reality of it.

Soon after Moffat's return to Cape Town, he received word from overseas that the parents of Mary Smith, his fiancé in England, had withdrawn their initial objections to them being married. After her arrival, they were married in Cape Town on 27th December 1819 and set off on their honeymoon, a 700-mile journey north by ox-wagon to a mission station called Lattakoo. The London Missionary Society directed Moffat to work among the Setswana-speaking people of that area.

There were many difficulties and disappointments. On one occasion they were blamed by a hostile crowd for the prevailing drought. Mothibi, the chief, had enlisted the assistance of a traditional rainmaker, but all to no avail. The missionaries were in danger; they were urged to leave or suffer the consequences. Moffat stood firm: 'We will not flee, for God has sent us and we are here to love and serve you in His name.'

In 1825 the Moffats moved to Kuruman, some eight miles distant, where there was a more reliable water supply from a perpetual spring. This would become their permanent home for many years. (Kuruman is presently a small town in the Northern Cape province of South Africa.) Progress seemed slow at first, but they worked hard. The tide seemed to turn in 1829 with a noticeable change in the attitude of the people to the message of the gospel. Moffat had earlier complained to his wife about the difficulties of the work and she had replied, 'We must not expect blessing till you are able, from your own lips and in their own language, to convey it through their ears into their hearts.' 'From that hour,' said Moffat, 'I gave myself with untiring diligence to the acquisition of the language.'

His greatest work must be regarded as the translation of the complete Scriptures into Setswana.[1] In 1825 small portions of scripture, a spelling-book, and catechism were prepared for printing in Cape Town. By mistake, these were sent on to England causing a major delay and great disappointment. By the end of 1829, Moffat had completed a translation of Luke's Gospel into Setswana. He travelled with this to Cape Town and initially found no suitable printing facilities. In the end, Sir Lowry Cole, the governor of the Cape, granted permission for the work to be produced at the Government Printing Office. However, Moffat had to typeset the whole text with his own hands under supervision. The work was completed in 1830.

He returned to Kuruman, bearing not only the precious translation of Luke's Gospel but also a small printing press that had originally been shipped out from England in 1825. It would give sterling service for many years. The first draft of the New Testament was completed in 1838 but this time, instead of it being printed at the Cape, Moffat and his family travelled to London for their first furlough, after 23 years of service. They bore the precious manuscript which was duly printed in 1840. On this visit to Britain, David Livingstone met Moffat for the first time. When the young missionary recruit sailed for Cape Town in 1841, Livingstone carried with him 500 copies of the new volume – the first New Testament in the language of any African people in southern Africa. The Moffats returned to Kuruman the next year.

The translation of the Old Testament was more difficult, but Moffat was assisted by his colleague, William Ashton, who had a working knowledge of Hebrew. Each book was printed on the small Kuruman press. Year after year their laborious efforts continued until 1857 when, at last, the whole Bible was completed, some 40 years after Moffat first arrived in Africa. 'When I had finished the last verse,' he wrote, 'a feeling came over me as if I should die. I fell upon my knees and thanked God for His wonderful grace in giving me strength to accomplish my task.'

Moffat retired from the mission field in 1870 and died in London in 1883. Even today in Botswana, we continue to thank God for one who persevered until he completed such a monumental task, making us the first people of southern Africa to have the whole Bible in our language. We still sing beautiful Setswana hymns that Moffat composed, and we continue to witness the power of the Word of God to change lives forever.

David Livingstone

David Livingstone

Accounts of the life and work of David Livingstone have resulted in enough volumes to fill a large library. They have ranged from Victorian hagiographies, in which a mere mortal is made out to be almost perfect, to modern revisionist accounts in which his every motive is impugned and his reputation is torn apart. Here we will confine ourselves to the known facts.

After meeting Moffat in Britain on his first furlough, Livingstone sailed for the Cape in 1840 under the auspices of the London Missionary Society. He brought with him a supply of the newly printed Setswana New Testament. He arrived as a single man and vowed to a friend that he preferred to remain that way.

Like so many others have done, Livingstone eventually reversed his strong opinions concerning matrimony. He recounted that on a visit to Kuruman, 'after nearly four years of African life as a bachelor, I screwed up courage to put a question beneath one of the fruit-trees, the result of which was that, in 1844, I became united in marriage to Mr Moffat's eldest daughter Mary'. In 1847 the couple moved further north to Kolobeng.[2] The new location was considered to be a suitable site for a mission station among the Bakwena. The area was soon afflicted by severe drought during 1848 and 1849. Livingstone wrote: 'Indeed, not 10 inches of water fell during these two years, and the Kolobeng ran dry; so many fish were killed that the hyenas from the whole country round collected to the feast and were unable to finish the putrid masses. A large old alligator [crocodile], which had never been known to commit any depredations, was found left high and dry in the mud among the victims.'

The chief of the Bakwena tribe was a man called Sechele. He is said to have been Livingstone's only known convert from that period. The rest of his tribe were at that time resistant to the message of the gospel and its implications for their lives. Sechele was a polygamist and traditional rainmaker. Professing faith in Christ meant that he was expected to renounce these customs. During the time of the profound drought, his profession of faith and his relationship with the missionary were put to the test – Livingstone's presence and his influence on the chief were being blamed for the lack of rain.

Livingstone was always on the move and in 1849, accompanied by his pregnant wife, he had made an arduous four-month trek even further north during which he discovered Lake Ngami. When they returned to Kolobeng, their fourth child, Elizabeth was born. She lived only about six weeks before succumbing to a respiratory illness. Livingstone wrote, 'We could not apply remedies to one so young, except the simplest. She uttered a piercing cry, and went away to see the King in His beauty. Here is the first grave in all that country marked as the resting-place of one … who shall live again.'

In 1851 Livingstone travelled north again and in May of the following year, Mary and the family were sent back to Britain. In their absence, an attack by marauding Boers resulted in their mission station at Kolobeng being completely ransacked. Their house was gutted, and all their possessions were wantonly destroyed or carried away. With a touch of humour, Livingstone wrote, 'They have taken away our sofa, I never had a good rest on it. Well, they can't have taken away all the stones.' Effectively the work at Kolobeng was finished and only the stones remained. The ruins of their mission station, about 20 miles from Gaborone, are there to this day. Down towards the riverbed are three grave mounds. The middle one is said to be that of Elizabeth Livingstone.

The local district hospital in the village of Molepolole, the Bakwena tribal capital, is known as the Scottish Livingstone Hospital. Outside the village, there is a cave situated on a steep cliff – Livingstone's Cave. It is said that one night he sheltered there with Sechele to help the chief overcome his fear of evil spirits.

Livingstone was aware of his personal limitations and failures when he wrote, 'I am a missionary, heart and soul' he insisted. 'God had an only Son, and He was a missionary and a physician. I am a poor, poor imitation of Him, or wish to be. In this service I hope to live; in it I wish to die!'

Khama 'The Great'

Khama 'The Great'

Khama III was the renowned Christian chief of the large Bamangwato tribe. His long life (c. 1837-1923) was filled with adventure, conflict, and danger. He was the eldest of the 16 sons of Sekgoma I. He stated that he became a Christian, not by the preaching of any missionary but by reading the Word of God: 'The teaching of the Word of God entered into my heart, and so I became a Christian believer' was his own simple and direct testimony. Until the day he died, no one was left in any doubt as to his convictions. He frequently stood alone against the tide of popular opinion in defence of the things he passionately believed.

In 1862, when he was about 25 years of age, Khama was baptised and soon afterwards he married Elisabeta Gobitsamang, a fellow believer. Later, 'on account of the Word of God', he refused his father's demands that he should take a second wife. Sekgoma was angered by his son's forthright stand against polygamy because he feared the loss of his authority as a chief, an authority that had always been demonstrated by the chief's leadership in traditional beliefs and practices.

That was only the beginning. In 1865, Khama refused to take part in the secret tribal initiation ceremonies which involved circumcision. He spoke out against the traditional rain-making ritual, immoral wedding celebrations, the bride-price, snuff-taking, buying on credit and many other concerns. He was strongly opposed to alcohol and was sometimes referred to as 'The Sniffer'. He declared, 'I am trying to lead my people according to the Word of God.'

He was a brave warrior, lithe, athletic and at least six feet tall. After numerous conflicts within the tribe, he became chief in 1875. Even when Sekgoma was embroiled in a bitter struggle with his son he said to his supporters: 'We think like this' tracing a circle in the sand, 'but Khama thinks like that', and he drew a straight line to indicate the integrity of his son. 'Khama doesn't lie' was how others described him.

In 1895, Khama was one of the three chiefs who travelled to Britain to visit Queen Victoria and seek protection against the expansionist designs of not only the Boers but also Cecil Rhodes. The latter saw Botswana as merely a land canal that would link up his imperialist ambitions for a Cape to Cairo monopoly on trade and commerce. It is said that Victoria presented Khama with a Bible inside which she inscribed these words: 'The secret of Khama's greatness.' The outcome of the historic meeting was that Botswana was made a British Protectorate.

Frederick Stanley Arnot

Frederick Stanley Arnot

Another Scotsman, F. S. Arnot was born in Glasgow in 1858. As a young boy, he heard David Livingstone speak on a visit to Britain. Impressions were made and desires were awakened that would bear fruit many years later. Arnot was converted when he was eleven. His interest in Africa did not wane and in 1881 he set sail for Cape Town. He had been commended to the grace of God by an assembly of Christians that gathered in Parkholm Hall in Glasgow.

His approach to missionary service would have been considered unconventional in his day. He was not trained at any theological institution, he was not ordained by any denominational church, he was not recruited or vetted by any mission board, and he was not guaranteed a salary or stipend by any organisation. However, what really mattered was that he was called and equipped by God to pioneer with the gospel in Africa.

Arnot's connection with Botswana is confined to a three-month period but it is significant for several reasons.[3] In 1882, on his journey further north, he stayed in the village of Shoshong which at that time was the capital of the Bamangwato tribe under their chief, Khama III. He arrived there on 11th March and apparently at first there was some reluctance to permit him to stay. He was not associated with the London Missionary Society whose personnel were in residence at that time. However, in the goodness of God, he was able to remain and over the next three months, he won the confidence of the people including Khama.

James Hepburn, the LMS missionary, taught Setswana to Arnot; he, in turn, gave English lessons to Hepburn's children. Arnot recalled a day when the unbelievers among the tribe were mocking 'the God of Khama and the Christians' for failing to give rain. The believers gathered outside to pray and, even as they prayed, the rain fell. Arnot himself commended the gospel by his manner of living. One day he trekked 24 miles to hunt for small game that would tempt the palate of a woman who had fallen sick in the village.

When it was time for Arnot to leave the royal capital and continue his journey, he packed his meagre possessions into six sailor's kitbags. He knew that he could never afford the lavish gifts that would be demanded by the Ndebele chief further north and so he chose to make a dangerous diversion through the Kalahari Desert. In an act of personal kindness and appreciation, the noble Khama lent Arnot his own ox-wagon and personal scout, Dinka, for the next leg of the journey.

On 8th June, Arnot gave a short farewell speech in Setswana. Ahead of him lay stirring adventures among the bushmen of the desert and a lifetime of service in the land of the Barotse. On the morning of his departure, he knew nothing of the future, but having just read Ephesians 5.25-29, he was encouraged afresh to trust the One who loves and cares for His own.

Arnot died on 15th May 1914, and Khama on 21st February 1923. On the Arnot memorial tombstone in Johannesburg are these words from Scripture: "In journeyings often" and "Thanks be to God which giveth us the victory through Jesus Christ our Lord". The inscription on Khama's tomb in Serowe is simpler still: "Righteousness exalteth a nation." The two men, both great and good, have met again.

F. S. Arnot was the first missionary in what would become a long line of men and women who came to Africa, believing and practising the Bible principles that still mark those whose labours in Botswana are described in this volume.

Alfred Merriweather

Dr Alfred Merriweather, our last individual of note, lived and worked in Botswana from his arrival in 1944 until his death in 1999. Born in Yorkshire in 1918, he grew up in Scotland and went to school and university in Edinburgh where he qualified in medicine.

He was associated with the Edinburgh Medical Missionary Society and the United Free Church of Scotland who ordained him as a preacher and sent him to Botswana as a missionary.

Alfred Merriweather
(With kind permission of Joy Crosbie,
nèe Merriweather)

Merriweather spent most of his life in the village of Molepolole, the capital of the Bakwena tribe, where he was the medical superintendent of the Scottish Livingstone Hospital. Despite having an outwardly quiet and unassuming manner, Merriweather earned deep respect throughout the country, even in government circles. He was known locally as 'RraBoitumelo' ('the father of Joy', his daughter) or sometimes called 'Rramosesane' ('the thin one').

Just before independence in 1966, Merriweather was appointed to be Speaker of the preparatory Legislative Council, going on to serve for several years as Speaker of the first National Assembly. He also became the personal physician to our first President,

Sir Seretse Khama. Merriweather was a faithful preacher of the gospel. He was fluent in Setswana and was often called upon to preach at gatherings, small or great. His years of working among the people he loved left him with a deep understanding of their minds and hearts.

In the early 1980s, health workers were constantly hearing the mantra 'Health for All by the Year 2000'. Public health officials throughout the world were arguing that within the context of the developing world, conventional western medicine could never hope to rise to meet all of the health needs on its own – it should work side by side with traditional doctors. Researchers from outside Botswana claimed that often traditional doctors were merely herbalists. Merriweather knew well, as did many Botswana Christians, that the distinction was not so clear cut. Underlying any visit to a traditional doctor was a fear of interference from the spirits of the ancestors and the remedy involved much more than taking herbs. While western doctors avoided using the word 'witchcraft' in their terminology, in case they sounded offensive, the people of Botswana had certainly not expunged the word *'boloi'* from their thinking or vocabulary.

The example Merriweather set meant that newly arrived people like ourselves, volunteer medical missionaries, were the better understood within government circles. They accepted that we were willing to contribute to the health needs of the people, but beyond that, they also recognised that we were committed to preaching the gospel.

Chapter 4

THE MISSIONARY MANDATE

For those who seek to serve God, their primary source of guidance is the Bible. Back in Old Testament times, in the reign of King Josiah, the temple had fallen into disrepair through neglect. Under layers of dust was found a book of the law (perhaps a scroll of Deuteronomy or the whole Pentateuch). It had been forgotten. However, when this book was recovered, read and heeded, the king and his people regained their clarity of vision and purpose which had been missing for so long (2 Kings 23.2-3).

This chapter aims to restate first principles that are often found buried beneath a heap of modern opinions and practices. We will focus on the Founder of Christianity, giving attention to what Christ said about His mission in this world and how He expected His servants to fulfil His purposes. The example of the first disciples in preaching the gospel, baptising converts, teaching the new believers, helping to establish local assemblies, shepherding the flock, and caring for each other is a thrilling story that pulsates with life, zeal and the warmth of Christ's love. Like ripples in a pond, the newly established Christian assemblies sought to reproduce the very same things they had been taught, and so the work grew and spread.

As mentioned previously, the convictions of those whose labours are described in this volume have been shaped by a desire to follow the Scriptures and to apply first-century principles to today's world. Are these principles still relevant and valid for today, or do they require an update to suit a modern world? Do they still work in a country such as Botswana?

The Command of Christ

'The Great Commission' is not a Bible term but it is often used to describe the risen Lord's parting words to His disciples. All four Gospels present the same command from a different viewpoint. Luke also adds further information at the beginning of his second volume, the Acts of the Apostles (all italics mine):

> And Jesus came and spake unto them, saying, *All power* is given unto me in heaven and in earth. Go ye therefore, and teach *all nations*, baptizing them in the name of the Father, and of the Son, and of the Holy Ghost: Teaching them to observe *all things* whatsoever I have commanded you: and, lo, I am with you *alway*, even unto the end of the world. Amen (Matthew 28.18-20).

> And he said unto them, Go ye into *all the world*, and preach the gospel to every creature (Mark 16.15).

> Then opened he their understanding, that they might understand the scriptures, And said unto them, Thus it is written, and thus it behoved Christ to suffer, and to rise from the dead the third day: And that repentance and remission of sins should be preached in his name among *all nations*, beginning at Jerusalem (Luke 24.45-47).

> Then said Jesus to them again, Peace be unto you: as my Father hath sent me, even so send I you (John 20.21).

But ye shall receive power, after that the Holy Ghost is come upon you: and ye shall be witnesses unto me both in Jerusalem, and in all Judaea, and in Samaria, and unto *the uttermost part of the earth* (Acts 1.8).

It is clear from these scriptures that the Lord Jesus Christ was issuing a command to His followers. He was sending them forth with His sovereign authority, enabling them by His Spirit, and also instructing them from His Word. They were to go into all the world and preach the gospel to every creature. No place and no person were to be overlooked; it was to be *anywhere and everywhere, to anyone and everyone.* His command applied not only to the disciples of His day but also to the followers of Christ in every age. That is why people have left their homeland, family and friends, to go to a foreign land such as Botswana and proclaim the gospel – God has called them, and they have responded.

Challenge

The gospel message confronts the status quo and for this reason God's servants require courage to be true and faithful. While the good news of the gospel should never be lost sight of, the initial diagnosis of man's condition strikes a mortal blow to any human pride or self-esteem.

In his treatise on the message of the gospel, the Epistle to the Romans, the apostle Paul began by exposing a state of universal guilt. In addressing both Gentiles and Jews, he reached several conclusions: there is no excuse – God has revealed Himself to all men (Romans 1.20); there is no escape – judgment is certain (Romans 2.3); there is no difference – all have sinned and fallen short of God's standard (Romans 3.22-23).

In today's world, the faithful evangelist will encounter resistance to this message. Many outwardly respectable people argue that, although they do not claim to be perfect, they are law-abiding, churchgoing, and neighbour-loving citizens. Their sincere hope is that they will accumulate enough good works to please God and gain an entrance into heaven. This common attitude is contrary to the gospel which presents the way of faith and not works, the principle of grace and not merit.

Another aspect of the gospel message presents Christ's exclusive claim to be the only way to God and the only Saviour of sinners. In a world of pluralism (there are many ways to God) and syncretism (where religion can be blended with traditional customs), every belief system is accommodated. Once again, the herald of the gospel will need boldness as well as compassion to present the truth.

Conflict

The proclamation of the gospel message has always been opposed. The Lord Jesus Christ suffered ridicule and finally a violent death at the prompting of the Jewish nation who refused His exclusive claims. His apostles were frequently imprisoned because they pressed home the sinner's guilt before God and God's love for the whole world, including the Gentiles. People resisted the stirring of their consciences, the challenge to their lifestyles, and the unmasking of their prejudices.

In the first century, those who had been Jews before becoming Christians were regarded as traitors by their unbelieving countrymen. They were considered to have abandoned their God-given religion to follow a discredited impostor called Jesus. Those who had been Gentiles before turning to Christ were perceived as a threat to the established order: quitting idolatry and immorality had a social impact which many unbelievers found gravely disturbing.

Coming to more recent times, men like Livingstone have been labelled as colonialists and little more than egotistical seekers after fame and fortune. Their names have been linked to subjugation and exploitation. They have been blamed for the loss of traditional cultural practices. They are accused of being paternalistic and stifling the local population. The common narrative today is that a sophisticated world no longer needs religion – religion is the problem rather than the solution.

The gospel has never been popular. Men travel the globe as politicians promising a better life, as businessmen advocating greater prosperity, as medical practitioners offering a new cure, and as educationalists proclaiming a higher way. Generally, they are welcomed with open arms. Let missionaries come with the message of the gospel – forgiveness and reconciliation, life and liberty, joy and peace, hope and assurance – and often they are viewed with suspicion.

Conversion

The gospel message will produce conversion in the lives of those who believe it. It transforms lives, as was seen so clearly in the life of Saul of Tarsus. A man who was motivated by hate became one who was constrained by love, a proud Pharisee became a humble disciple of Christ, and a persecutor and murderer became a tender shepherd of God's people who devoted the rest of his life to tending the flock.

Furthermore, the power of the gospel is such as to change societies in a radical way. The enemies of the gospel charged the early preachers of having "turned the world upside down" (Acts 17.6).

Yes, it happened then and still does today: a drunkard stops beating his wife and begins to provide for the family he has neglected; an adulterous man becomes a faithful and loving husband; a crooked businessman become honest and starts paying his taxes; an unscrupulous boss starts treating his workers with dignity and fairness; a troubled teenager finds hope and a purpose for living … The list is endless. The gospel transforms lives from the inside out.

Conversions are not welcomed by everyone. The book of the Acts relates how the new believers in Ephesus turned to Christ from idolatry. A public renunciation of their old ways culminated in them burning their books of spells. The threat to the commerce of the city, and in particular the lucrative silversmith's trade of selling images of the goddess, Diana, resulted in the enemies of the gospel inciting a riot (Acts 19.23-30). When vested interests are challenged, they can respond forcefully with antagonism. The early church was persecuted for many such reasons. By God's grace, even those who fled for their lives did not cease to testify of their faith in Christ, and so the word was spread afar (Acts 8.4). God's purposes cannot be stayed; they can only be redirected.

Continuity

Those who believed in Christ were to be baptised and taught to be obedient to the Word of God. Anticipating the difficulties that lay ahead of His disciples, the Lord promised that He would always be with them in the work. They were not alone. This precious promise has fortified and comforted His followers through the centuries.

Christ's commands indicated that after preaching the gospel, the conversion of souls was not the endpoint. New converts were not to be abandoned; they were to be cared for, shepherded, and taught the whole counsel of God. This would keep anyone busy for a lifetime. The first Christians got off to a good start, but they kept going and "continued stedfastly in the apostles' doctrine and fellowship, and in breaking of bread, and in prayers" (Acts 2.42).

When the Lord Jesus declared that "I will build my church" (Matthew 16.18) and used the word "church" for the first time, He was not referring to a religious building such as a cathedral, or even a modern-day Christian denomination. The word refers to all believers in this age of grace who have been called out of the world. The frequently used word, 'assembly', when applied to a local company of such Christians, perhaps comes closest to this fundamental meaning. They gather together in His Name alone (Matthew 18.20).

The record of Dr Luke in the Acts of the Apostles, and the letters written by the apostle Paul and others gave guidance and direction to the first local churches. Taking heed to the principles of the Word of God would bring glory to Him, honour to Christ, and blessing to others.

A Local Assembly of Christians

JOY IN THE DESERT

Characteristics of a Local Church

How did the first Christians practise their faith? Some distinctive features will be listed and expanded briefly. The Bible references in support of these practices are too numerous to list here in full; only a selection of key references follows:

1. **The Centrality of Christ.** They bore His Name alone and understood Him to be the Head of the Church which is His body (Colossians 1.18). They sought to honour Him and be obedient to His word in all that they did. Any desire to divide into separate groups and align themselves with prominent men like Paul and Apollos was resisted (1 Corinthians 1.10-13).

2. **The Veracity of the Bible.** It was their only handbook, and 'What saith the Scriptures?' was the sole criterion in deciding any course of action. Individual believers were taught the need of a private time alone with God each day, reading the Bible for themselves and speaking to God in prayer. They were taught the Scriptures regularly and comprehensively so that they manifested spiritual growth and maturity (2 Timothy 3.16-17).

3. **The Autonomy of each Local Church.** Each assembly of Christians was genuinely self-governing, self-supporting and self-propagating. There was no hierarchy and no controlling 'mother church' or ruling headquarters deciding policy for the rest. Each would be equally accountable to Christ (Revelation 1.13, 20). Even though the work began in Jerusalem, the centre of Judaism, it spread rapidly throughout the known world and took root in many Gentile towns and cities.

4. **The Plurality of Elders.** Each assembly was led by a group of godly men with shepherd hearts who worked among the

people and constantly cared for them. They were also referred to as "overseers" (Acts 20.17, 28); they shared in all of the responsibilities and were mutually accountable. They made sure that the needs of the flock were met by guiding, teaching, encouraging, correcting, and protecting the believers under their care.

5. **The Variety of Gifts.** Every believer has received a gift from God and the indwelling Spirit of God enables them to exercise and express that gift (1 Corinthians 12.4-7). Not all gifts are public. Many are exercised behind the scenes, but they are just as important as the more obvious gifts of preaching and teaching. Gifts are exercised to honour the Lord and also to build up His church. They are not given for self-glory or self-enrichment.

6. **The Liberty of Priesthood**. Every believer, male and female, has the privilege of directly worshipping God (1 Peter 2.5, 9). As shown above, each is also expected to serve God in the use of their gifts. Men are to take the lead publicly; women have a different role. In the gatherings of a local church, men uncover their heads and audibly worship; women cover their heads and silently worship (1 Corinthians 11.1-16; 1 Timothy 2.11-12). They are of equal importance and they complement one another as together they honour their Lord by being obedient to His Word.

7. **The Unity of Purpose.** When Christians are united, they are strong and effective (Philippians 1.27). The local assembly exists for three main reasons: to worship and serve God; to encourage and build up one another; and to pray for and reach out to the lost. The upward, inward, and outward

perspectives are all important. Any imbalance will result ultimately in spiritual impoverishment and loss.

8. **The Primacy of Preaching.** Gospel activity is a manifestation of love for those who will perish in their sins if they do not trust Christ the Saviour. An inward-looking and self-centred church becomes 'a holy huddle'. Without engaging wholeheartedly in evangelism, it is doomed to die out. Every believer is to be a missionary in his or her locality, spreading the word in conversation to one and all. The pioneer evangelist reaches out to new areas where he publicly declares the message (2 Timothy 4.2).

9. **The Responsibility of Teaching.** New Christians need spiritual food – the milk of the Word. Mature Christians need the meat of the Word. A local church should provide a balanced diet that caters for all (Acts 20.27-28). Reading, studying and understanding the Bible is only the prelude to practising its commands. Bible students call these three principles observation, interpretation, and application. We are to be doers of the Word and not hearers only (James 1.22).

10. **The Necessity of Caring.** Love is the mortar or glue that binds Christians together. Orthodoxy in doctrine and busyness in service are never enough. Believers have divine love poured into them so that it will flow out of them. The first Christians loved and cared for one another and supported those who were needy (Acts 2.44-47). Their love also overflowed to the surrounding communities. They were known as people who were kind. They represented a giving God by being those who selflessly sacrificed their time, energy and resources to honour and serve Him.

Conclusion

The record in the following pages is of God's blessing on the service of men and women from overseas and from within Botswana whom God has called first to salvation and then to service. They share the same convictions and desire only to be faithful to God and His Word, seeking to practise the principles of their faith as did the first Christians. These first-century principles still work in our modern world, but they do require confidence in God and personal commitment. Many of these are now outside the realm of popular religion and appear to some people as being antiquated and irrelevant. We have not found that to be the case: the joy and power of transformed lives tell their own story.

Does this mean that when Christians do their best to practise these principles, everything falls into place and runs smoothly? Far from it. Difficulties often confront those who desire to be faithful to God's Word. Problems arise, not because of the divine principles – they will always hold good – but because of our own human frailty.

Whenever and wherever God is blessing, the devil always counterattacks. He is busy seeking to divide believers, attacking from the outside and disturbing on the inside. He aims to discourage them through opposition, disturb them with false teaching, or defile them through unholy living.

Over the years there have been perplexing challenges in the service of God. We can look back and thank God for the measure of preservation due to His grace alone. At times we have had to admit our own weakness and failure. What does the Lord require of us, "but to do justly, and to love mercy, and to walk humbly with [our] God?" (Micah 6.8).

Chapter 5

BEGINNINGS

Botswana gained its independence in 1966. At midnight on 30th September, the British Union Jack was lowered for the last time and the new Botswana flag was hoisted. The story goes that the flag was slow to unfurl until a providential gust of wind aided the process and the distinctive blue, black and white colours were on full display for the first time. As noted previously, the colour blue signified rain (*pula*), a precious resource in a desert land. 'Pula!' is the celebratory cry of the people of Botswana as well as being the name of our currency. Our newly adopted national anthem sounded out loud and clear: *Fatshe leno la rona, Ke mpho ya Modimo* (Blessed be this noble land, Gift to us from God's strong hand). A further blessing from above was also welcome – it began to rain. Pula!

The Call of God

Across the seas, 1966 was also an important year for a young Scottish couple who had just been married. Jim Legge grew up in Fife and was saved in his early teens. Those who influenced his spiritual development were his older brother, Alec, and men such as Willie Scott of Machermore Castle, W. W. Fereday, and Albert Leckie. Jim's love for the Scriptures and zeal in gospel activity were nurtured at that time. After schooling in Lochgelly, he completed an apprenticeship as a baker. Later, as a conscientious objector, he began training to become a registered male nurse. Soon afterwards he met a young lady, Irene Kent, who was also nursing at Dunfermline West Fife Hospital. Unlike Jim, Irene did not have a Christian family background, but she too had trusted Christ as her personal Saviour. A notable feature of those years was Jim's bold witness for Christ that resulted in nursing colleagues being saved.

By the time Jim and Irene were married in 1966, they already shared the conviction that God was calling them to Africa to serve Him there for the rest of their lives. With the commendation of the Cowdenbeath assembly, they left for Portugal on honeymoon to learn Portuguese, hoping to proceed onwards to Angola. Their language teacher was Viriato Sobral of Espinho. When the door to Angola closed, they did not give up. They moved to Zimbabwe (then Southern Rhodesia) with a view to pioneering with the gospel in Malawi, but again, with the refusal of a visa, the door did not open.

Viewing the Land

Crawford Allison and George Wiseman, originally missionaries in Angola, were at that time based in Salisbury, Rhodesia (later known as Harare, Zimbabwe). In 1967 they made an exploratory visit to Botswana. Crawford Allison wrote in his memoirs, *Leaves from the African Jungle*, of sitting around their campfire and interacting with the local bushmen who had paid them an unexpected visit. These two experienced servants of God considered that the country was open for the spread of the gospel. This was encouraging news for Jim and Irene to hear.

The next year, Crawford and George visited Botswana again, this time accompanied by Jim and Irene, Walter Gammon and Tommy Meeney. In the capital, Gaborone, they were able to meet Winifred Wickendon, a Christian lady who formerly was associated with an assembly of believers in Gravesend, England. Miss Wickendon was employed in the British High Commission and she was able to facilitate meetings with government officials. She was helpful in every way. The outcome was that Jim and Irene were granted permission to engage in medical work and assigned a small government house for rent in the village of Serowe, some 200 miles away. They felt that this location would afford them a better chance of learning to speak Setswana. Crawford Allison, a bricklayer by trade who became an outstanding African linguist, had been able to teach them basic Setswana. But apart from that, and the acquisition of the grammar book we would all come to know well (*Introduction to Tswana* by Alexander Sandilands), at the beginning they were on their own.

The Legge Family

Laying a Foundation

When Jim moved around the village many children would run up to him excitedly and say, '*Ke kopa siki.*' This occurred so often that Jim reckoned this must be the normal greeting and he put it to full use. One day a local pastor, Martin Morolong, enlightened him: the children were actually saying, 'I am asking for sixpence!' Martin was able to spend some time with Jim and Irene, assisting them in learning the language. Their children, Judith and Crawford, played with the local boys and girls and, as children do, they soon picked up the language with much greater ease than their parents. Jim and Irene persisted in mastering Setswana. They became fluent speakers and ardent lovers of the language.

One of the first things Jim did was to approach the leaders of the village with regard to providing some medical help in the village. Rre Kgamane arranged a meeting with several members of the royal family, Kgosi Mokgacha Mokgadi and Rre Lenyeletse Seretse. (*Rre* is a term of respect for an older man, meaning 'my father'; *Kgosi* means 'Chief'.) They granted Jim permission to begin a clinic but they also made clear that the government was not in a position to provide funding. This was not of any major concern to Jim who was trusting in the Lord for all his needs; however, a classroom was made available at Khama Memorial School.

This early clinic work resulted in Jim meeting with an elderly patient, Rre Gaolekwe Lekoko. He became one of the first converts. He was literally an old soldier, having fought with the Allies in North Africa in the Second World War. Any time he was photographed, though short of stature, he would stand smartly to attention, unsmiling, and with his arms straight down by his sides, as if on parade. After trusting Christ, Rre Lekoko disposed of all his cattle, leaving himself free to attend the assembly meetings. He lived in humble circumstances, a small thatched hut, and remained one of the most faithful believers, right up until his homecall. At the end of a Bible conference in those early days, he would always request we sing his favourite hymn – *Re tlaa rakana* (God be with you till we meet again).

Rre Lekoko

A few months later Rre Kgamane himself came to the clinic with a severe toothache and Jim was able to deal with it. Not long after that, permission was granted to extend the clinic services to other outlying villages, namely Paje, Tshimoyapula, and Mabeleapodi. Every Monday and Wednesday became the clinic days when, assisted by their domestic helper, Miss Grace Ntlole, Jim and Irene took their children along, packed up their truck with medical supplies and food, and headed down the sandy bush road.

They sometimes slept in the clinic building in the villages, especially in bad weather or if they finished work late. Jim would use this opportunity to invite the patients and their family members back to the clinic for an evening gospel meeting. On one occasion after heavy rain, their Landcruiser, even with four-wheel drive, got deeply stuck in the mud. They had to camp in the bush for several days until a tractor arrived to tow them out.

In the village of Serowe, Jim had at first rented a property to serve as a small office and bookroom. Having been so greatly influenced by Crawford Allison, Jim and Irene began preparing gospel literature in Setswana. Initially, they were assisted by Dr Merriweather in Molepolole who arranged for the material to be translated. Later they were themselves able to translate Bible courses and other booklets that they felt would be useful in their work.

Serowe Gospel Hall

Every day, on their way from their house to the village centre, Jim and Irene passed a small church building by the side of the road. It had been erected in 1950 to serve the sizeable English-speaking community but with the decline in their numbers, it had fallen into disuse as a church. The expatriates and traders had used it as a day school for their younger children. It also had been a venue for tea parties where the womenfolk raised funds for various charitable projects such as the building of the Lady Khama community hall in the village. One day Irene asked the postmistress, Miss Audrey Blackbeard, about the church building. She was able to arrange a meeting with the trustees. Among those who attended were local businessmen and European traders; a few others who attended had hopes of using the building for a local company of Scouts.

Ntlo ya Efangele

On the day of the meeting, as the discussion proceeded, a prominent businessman called Billy Woodford said, 'I suggest that we give the Legges the hall for five Rands.' Jim bowed his head and silently prayed, knowing he did not have the amount at that time. Just then Gwen Blackbeard, Audrey's mother, stood up and said to the others, 'Who does this house belong to? Can we sell the house of the Lord? I suggest that we give Jim Legge this hall for free to use for the Lord's work.' Thus they got the hall without having to pay anything. The one condition was that they should assist in funeral services and burials of local business folk who were no longer associated with any of the denominational churches in the village. The small church building became known as *Ntlo ya Efangele ya Serowe* (Serowe Gospel Hall).

The Assembly Commences

At first, when they held a meeting in the hall, Irene would stand outside with tracts, inviting passers-by to come in; Jim would be inside preaching the gospel in Setswana to a few souls. An office and clinical storeroom were erected on the large plot and in later years classrooms and ablution blocks were added to accommodate the growing Sunday School. These extra rooms also provided sleeping quarters for the visiting believers during conference times. A local brother, Onkutule Rannau, assisted in the building work. An electrician known only as 'Mr Time' and a welder from the village, Tom Lottering, were also involved.

Through the gospel witness in the village, several people professed faith in Christ and these were subsequently baptised in a friend's swimming pool. Later, a makeshift metal tank was used on the hall site. In 1970 the small assembly of believers began breaking bread to remember the Lord. This early progress was sadly brought to an abrupt halt, almost overnight, when it came to light that several members of the assembly had to be put out of the fellowship because of sin. Jim and Irene had to pick themselves up and start again. Jim would write later about the difficulties of those early years: 'We did not know the customs of the people and many mistakes were made. But out of it all there are those who are a constant source of encouragement to us and they have gone on in spite of very severe trials to their faith'.

Early Converts

One of the early converts was a young woman, Mavis Medupe, who was training to be a nurse. She spent three years at Sekgoma Memorial Hospital in Serowe, from 1971-1973. Mavis became not only a close friend to the Legges but also, from the beginning, she proved to be an ardent soul-winner. During her training, she taught memory verses to the children who were hospitalised for long periods of time. She also helped Jim and Irene with their Sunday School. From that time in her life, she recalls that she learned to trust in the Lord with all her heart (Proverbs 3.5-6).

When her father was killed in a car accident and her young brother died of tuberculosis, Mavis was under great pressure from the family to take part in traditional practices, seeking protection from *badimo* (the spirits of the ancestors). She refused. This and other trials came her way because of her faith in the Lord.

When she moved to Francistown for midwifery training, she was encouraged in her spiritual growth by Ian and Rebecca Rees who gave her a study Bible. Again she was involved in their Sunday School. Her next stop was the large town of Mahalapye where there is no assembly to this day. She had a class there of about 30 children. For the next 23 years she nursed in the mine hospital in Jwaneng, many miles away from fellowship with other believers; nevertheless, she used her home for a large Sunday School. At the end of each year, she invited different brethren to assist her at the prize-giving time and to preach the gospel.

Mavis has now retired to her home village of Shoshong but her zeal has not dimmed. Several young people have been saved and are now in assembly fellowship elsewhere. Year by year she has organised a study week and gospel activities. In more recent years she has invited brethren from Gaborone and Francistown to assist with Bible teaching. Brethren from Serowe and Palapye are nearer to hand and continue to help on a more regular basis. Mavis continues to enjoy the truth of the Bible and cites two verses (1 Corinthians15.58 and 2 Corinthians 9.6) as being her current favourites: keep abounding in the work of the Lord and sow bountifully.

Another notable contact from those years was a young man called Kgosi Mompati. He had grown up in Serowe and spent his boyhood herding his father's cattle. He started school when he was 11 years of age but soon caught up. A South African evangelist visited his school and Kgosi trusted Christ as his Saviour in 1972. However, he lacked assurance and knew little of the truth of the eternal security of the believer. As a consequence, he had doubts about his salvation. He was also interested in baptism but knew little about it. Other acquaintances were putting pressure on him to speak in tongues, to be baptised to complete his salvation, or to keep the Sabbath day. By God's grace and providence, it was then that he came to meet Jim and Irene Legge. His many questions were answered and his doubts were dispelled. It was with great joy in December 1973, that he and Rre Lekoko were baptised and then received into assembly fellowship in Serowe. There were then seven believers in fellowship.

Kgosi's life would take several unusual turns over the next few years. After initial studies at the university in Gaborone, he was sent to study medicine at the renowned Makerere University in Kampala, Uganda. It was at that time that Idi Amin came to power and student life became difficult in Uganda. Food was scarce and even basic supplies such as soap were unavailable. Kgosi's Botswana sponsors had also delayed to send him the necessary funds for his living expenses. He could only trust in the Lord who faithfully sustained him. Time and again his needs were met at the last moment by local friends, believers in Botswana, and even praying Christians overseas.

In 1976, after a brief holiday back home in Botswana, Kgosi was returning to Uganda via Kenya. On arrival at Nairobi airport, he discovered that his bag containing everything he needed was missing. He spent a few days in Nairobi, staying with a friendly Christian couple he knew, waiting for the bag to turn up. Had he proceeded on his journey as scheduled, he would have been caught up in the famous raid on Entebbe airport, when Israeli commandos rescued hostages from a hijacked Air France aeroplane.

Idi Amin was already seething with anger at countries such as Botswana that had boycotted a summit of the OAU (Organisation of African Unity) at which Amin was to be showcased as chairman for that year. He accused these countries of being traitors. Following the further humiliation of the Entebbe raid, a lowly Motswana medical student might easily have suffered the wrath of the rattled Ugandan security forces. The Lord preserved Kgosi at that time. On the orders of Amin, 245 Kenyans including airport staff were murdered in retaliation for Kenya's assistance to Israel. Over 3,000 Kenyans living and working in Uganda fled to their homeland.

The Botswana government wisely transferred its medical students to Nairobi. A missionary couple from overseas, John and Yokey Roberts, as well as a local couple, Robert and Rose Gitau, were a great help to Kgosi and his close student friend from Botswana, Dorcas Molefi. Kgosi and Dorcas would later be joined in marriage and continue to encourage one another in serving the Lord. After qualifying in medicine and being posted to Gaborone, Kgosi and Dorcas's home became a convenient place for a small number of like-minded believers to meet.

The Mompati Family

Help and Progress

In 1973 a sister from the UK, Miss Irene Stretch, joined the work in Serowe. She remained in Botswana before returning to Scotland in 1976 on medical grounds. In several short reports published in a missionary magazine, she spoke of her efforts to learn the language and also of opportunities she had to witness to those attending the Teacher Training College in Serowe.

Many other people came to faith in Christ including large families in which nearly every member was saved. Even when these early converts were transferred away from Serowe because of their schooling or employment, they maintained contact with Jim and Irene who encouraged them to continue sowing the seed of the Word of God. Ivan and Lenyora Mbangiwa were based in one of the outlying villages where Ivan was a schoolteacher and Lenyora had been a Family Welfare Educator in a local government clinic. They maintained a testimony wherever they worked. Ivan was from the Kalanga tribe and so Setswana was not his first language. He would later become a headmaster in Nata, much further north.

In a letter Jim wrote to me in 1977, he mentioned another one of their clinics, '52 miles away in the back of beyond ... the area is a forsaken one ... semi-desert, and not one iota of development has taken place. The people are untouched by the gospel and thus a great challenge is placed before us. Brother, would you pray that it might please the Lord to raise up those specifically called and equipped to pioneer in an area like this.' This was the spirit of the gospel pioneer that marked Jim all of his days.

Step by step the work grew and the believers in the assembly became more involved in serving the Lord. The gifts of preaching the gospel and teaching the Word of God were nurtured as well as the responsibility of all to be soul-winners. The Lord began to raise up godly local men with caring hearts to share in leadership and shepherding the flock. From the beginning, Jim and Irene were hard-working, disciplined and organised, setting the tone for what would follow. God blessed these efforts for His glory.

Chapter 6

SEROWE

The work in Serowe continued to grow steadily. Throughout the 70s, the various reports that Jim and Irene Legge sent back to the UK told of the widening circle of contacts in Serowe and outlying villages. Opportunities began to open up to preach the gospel in other locations such as the schools, clinics, the local hospital and prisons.

Before they were given the small church building that became the Gospel Hall, they had used a school classroom for regular meetings. The small office they began renting in the village doubled as a bookshop. They made extensive use of Emmaus courses to maintain a regular link with those who asked for literature and were keen to study the Scriptures. The first Setswana tracts and booklets were translated and subsequently printed by the Mission Press in Bellville, South Africa.

After the clinic work commenced in 1971, four outlying villages were visited regularly. The local schoolchildren could be visited the same day. Sometimes a meeting for adults was held in the clinic building in the evening. Reports published in *Medical Missionary News* highlighted the health challenges of those years: malnutrition, childhood infections, inadequate antenatal care, and tuberculosis.

Their first believer's conference was attended by only a few local people. One small three-legged cooking pot was all that was required to cater for those who came. The numbers would quickly increase, year upon year, and soon several more larger cooking pots were required. Visits from respected and experienced brethren such as the late Gordon Jones (Zaire), Crawford Allison (Angola and Zimbabwe), Boyd Nicholson (Canada) and T. Ernest Wilson (Angola and USA) were appreciated. There were also several African evangelists, Simon Ndlovu and Edward Maphosa, and other brethren from South Africa who gave help at such times. Often people were saved during these special times of fellowship, preaching and teaching. New believers would be baptised in public testimony to their faith in the Lord Jesus Christ.

The Lord raised up godly men and women in the Serowe assembly who have remained faithful to the truths they were taught. It was there that they were saved and nurtured in the faith. Because of the needs of further education or employment, many believers have been transferred from Serowe to other places where they have continued to be a blessing to the assembly work throughout Botswana.

Serowe would become the home of new missionary couples and their families for varying periods whose priority was to learn the language and culture, while assisting the growing assembly work in the village. The Logans from Belfast were there from 1982-84 before moving to Gaborone; the Rees family from Bath spent 1984-85 in Serowe before moving to Francistown; the Raggetts from Manchester stayed from 1992-99, before moving to Palapye; and the last couple to reside in the village from 2007-2010 were the McIlroys from Kells, Northern Ireland, who would later relocate to Maun.

Teaching a new language requires commitment and patience. Time must be set aside for regular lessons, and then there are also exercises to be corrected and returned. Jim and Irene's goal was that each new missionary couple should be able to communicate the gospel to others in Setswana. In their already busy routine, the Legges made the necessary sacrifices to assist us all to get off to a good start.

The Logans

Both Hazel and I were saved and called young in life. It was the same gospel preacher, Sammy Thompson, who pointed us both to Christ. As a young boy, hearing T. Ernest Wilson speak about Angola stirred me. Hazel heard the call of God when she was 13, after listening to Tom Bentley of Malaysia speak on Romans 12.1 at a missionary conference. We met some years later at a missionary study class in Belfast. It was on a visit to Ayrshire in Scotland that I picked up a prayer leaflet and read for the first time of the labours of Jim and Irene. We began corresponding and Hazel and I met them on one of their furloughs. We were able to pay a short visit to Botswana in 1980. Everything about the country fascinated us. On one memorable evening in Jim and Irene's home in Serowe we had a joint celebration – it was their 14th wedding anniversary and our first! Two years later, we returned to join them, having been commended by the Dundonald assembly in Northern Ireland. By that time, we carried our two-month old daughter in our arms. Heather was soon given a Setswana name – *Sethunya* (the flower). I then became *RraSethunya* and Hazel became *MmaSethunya*, the father and mother of 'the flower'. These will be our names for all our days in Botswana.

In 1982, the assembly in Serowe was still small but one quickly sensed that a solid foundation had been faithfully laid. We started language study and began to help with the clinic work and the assembly activities. It was a privilege to work together with Jim and Irene and also it was a joy to start getting to know the local believers. After three months, I delivered my first gospel message in Setswana. It had taken many hours to prepare, but when it was preached (read), it lasted all of five minutes. Hazel became adept at conversational Setswana and could speak with anyone about anything.

Jim and Irene had arranged a rental house for us nearby to their home, a prefabricated building with a tin roof and panelled walls. There were already residents living there – a large family of lizards – and they remained, generously sharing their accommodation with us for the next two years. Other adventures lay ahead. We soon discovered another family, this time mice, living in our oven. The snake that slithered out of our bedroom one evening was quickly dispatched by Hazel using two kitchen knives. The scorpion that was found amongst my books was shown the door, whereas the huge, hairy rain spider scurrying around the bathroom was shown no mercy. At that time, there was no electricity in Serowe, so at night we used gas lamps. Had we opened the windows, we would have been invaded by swarms of insects. Being in the middle of a prolonged drought, the heat was extreme, and under our hot tin roof, we cooked!

Our water supply came from a borehole. We tried to maintain the garden of the property with its fruit trees bearing naartjies, lemons, guavas, pomegranates and mulberries. Our early attempts at home gardening yielded a good crop of cauliflowers and cabbages, but most other vegetables struggled to grow in the heat. Without refrigeration, fresh produce was hard to come by. We got to know that the local butcher had a new supply of meat when he displayed the cow's head in a wheelbarrow outside his front door. A few hens and ducks as well as a black Labrador, Emma, completed our family.

We learned so many valuable lessons from Jim and Irene. Jim was an early riser, spending time alone with God. Later in the morning, they would 'go to work', whether it was out to the village clinics or down to their office. Hazel and I both enjoyed being able to help in the medical work and travelling out together with them to the village clinics twice a week. I preached with Jim in the assembly hall, in prisons, and in schools. We saw their passion for the gospel and its proclamation. I also recall Jim's careful and patient teaching of the Word, as he instructed the little group of believers and ourselves. He would occasionally assist me when I was called to the local hospital to deal with a difficult obstetric case requiring surgery. When he needed surgery on his infected finger, I performed it. When I needed surgery on my lacerated finger, he performed it. We both bore the scars to prove it.

Several months before moving to Gaborone, our son, Andrew, was born in the local Sekgoma Memorial Hospital. We called him after his two grandfathers – Andrew Edward – but one of the believers chose another name for him: *Kgosietsile*, which means 'the chief has come'.

The Reeses

Ian and Rebecca Rees were commended to the Lord's work in Botswana in 1984 by the assemblies at Manvers Hall in Bath and Treboeth in Swansea. After qualifying in law, Ian worked for a time at Echoes of Service in Bath where he became familiar with many missionaries and their work. Rebecca had finished training in Domestic Science shortly before her marriage. Together with their infant son, Adam, they arrived in 1984 and settled into a house in the centre of the village of Serowe where they too set about learning Setswana. They were able to provide cover for Jim and Irene when they went on furlough and also for ourselves when we were away. By that time, we had moved to Gaborone and Ian came to stay in our home and keep the work going when we were overseas. After two years in Serowe, they moved to Francistown to open up the work there.

Ian was keen to learn more of the language and together we enrolled to do further Setswana studies by correspondence with the University of South Africa based in Pretoria. Their well-organised courses included challenging assignments that we had to complete and post back to our tutors. We were also exposed to Setswana literature and poetry. After moving to Francistown, Ian continued his interest in literature and translation work and opened a Bible bookshop in the town.

The Raggetts

Of all the couples who began their service in Serowe, Colin and Christine Raggett spent the longest time there, from 1992 to 1999. They had been commended by two assemblies in Manchester. After moving to Palapye to further the new work there, they continued to be part of the Serowe assembly until they began to meet as a new assembly in Palapye in 2003.

They were fully involved in all aspects of the work in Serowe and were privileged to witness and share in the rapid expansion of the assembly itself, the Sunday School and correspondence work throughout the 90s. At one time about 1,000 children were attending the Serowe Sunday School and 100 young men and women were in the Bible Class. Due to health problems, Jim and Irene had both retired from clinical work. Subsequently, they devoted their time and effort to building up the literature work and organising a print room where they could conveniently produce tracts and Bible lessons.

Colin accompanied Jim on his visits to believer's homes, outlying villages, schools and prisons. There were opportunities to preach at the prisons twice a week. Funerals, as already described, are an important social event in the life of Batswana. The week of prayers each evening before the day of the burial would see dozens of people attending and listening to a short message from the Bible. With the HIV epidemic, there were frequent funerals in Serowe. Jim always used these opportunities to present the gospel, sharing the preaching with Colin and other brethren who accompanied him. Apart from assembly activities, Christine was kept busy with the homeschooling of her three children. Having trained as a teacher, she was well qualified for the task.

There were profitable series of gospel tent meetings in those years and Jim and Colin shared the preaching. The month of September was considered to be the best month – not too hot and not too cold, as well as being not too wet. The large tent was often filled and apart from one incident when some ropes were found to have been cut during the night, there were no problems with vandalism. In addition to these meetings, other spells of gospel preaching took place in different home yards in the village. There were few slack days and practical skills were often required for various building and maintenance projects.

The work in schools expanded when Colin obtained permission to speak each week to all of the five Junior Secondary Schools in Serowe. Following this, the door opened up for the 17 Primary Schools to be visited and the most senior classes, Standards four to seven, continued to hear the Word of God. Even after the syllabus was changed, Colin still had the liberty to continue with Bible teaching.

Missionary Families

The McIlroys

Franklin and Jenny McIlroy had been commended by the Kells assembly in Northern Ireland. They had already made a short visit to Botswana before they returned in December of 2007 with their three children to begin missionary service. It is worth noting that Franklin's initial application for a residence permit was turned down. This had never happened before. The reason given was that he and his wife were not 'ordained ministers of religion'. A letter of appeal from Jim Legge and myself, accompanied by much prayer, was eventually successful. Franklin's training and experience in the construction business were ideally suited for their time in Serowe. Apart from the obligatory and vital language study, he was able to assist in the erection of a new hall in another area of Serowe, Goora-Leina.

The new hall was completed in 2008 in a developing area of the village and three weeks of gospel meetings resulted in two teenagers trusting Christ. A regular gospel witness continued weekly and a Sunday School was commenced. As with other brethren who had previously assisted Jim in gospel work, Franklin was able to begin preaching and teaching the Word, not only in the two Serowe halls but also in the Junior Secondary Schools in the village. Hundreds of children as well as their teachers were exposed to the gospel. The good attendances at both the Sunday School and Bible Class resulted in other young men and women coming to faith in Christ, year by year. Franklin also linked up with Colin to have gospel meetings in a home yard in Mahalapye.

In December of 2009, a notable baptism took place. Eight believers were baptised in Serowe including RraKole, a man who had double amputations of his lower limbs. Since trusting Christ, this brother has been a constant source of encouragement to the believers in Serowe. He lives outside the village, but arrangements are made to collect him as often as possible for the assembly meetings and then take him home afterwards.

Franklin was also able to help in the literature work with the introduction of two-colour Riso printing. He recalls that in 2009, around 450,000 tracts and Bible lessons were printed. Each week tracts were distributed in the local hospital. Other items such as gospel calendars were produced and some of the older materials were revised and upgraded. A Setswana version of a gospel booklet, *Vital Questions* by Clifford Law, was prepared and printed in Gaborone. These were widely distributed amongst the assemblies.

Good teaching books were ordered from overseas and a bookstall became a welcome feature of our various conferences. Franklin also prepared Scripture texts in Setswana in various sizes. Messages were recorded at our conferences and a series of CDs were made available to the believers. Joe Skelly of Northern Ireland gave valuable assistance in setting this up. These CDs covered a wide range of Bible ministry topics and also gave the opportunity to include messages from well-known overseas speakers.

In 2008, a serious accident had occurred in Serowe. A fully laden construction truck sped down the nearby hill next to the Gospel Hall and veered off the road, crashing through the wall of the office. The two young women who were working there at the time were covered in rubble. In the mercy of God, their lives were spared; however, they did take some time to recover from their injuries and the psychological trauma of this incident.

Office Damage

Franklin was able to assist in the rebuilding and refurbishing of the office. A strong, protective outer wall was also constructed. The owner of the truck company could not deny liability, but he never offered to pay for the damage.

In August of 2010, Franklin and Jenny and their growing family moved to Maun to help in the work there. Sid and Karen Halsband from Canada had pioneered in Maun but were unable to continue there due to Sid's deteriorating physical condition (see Chapter 10).

Sudden Changes

Young boys and girls who were saved at Sunday School in Serowe grew up to become adult Christian men and women. What was even more pleasing was to witness their spiritual growth and care for others. Jim and Irene had been training and encouraging these brethren and sisters for some years to share in various aspects of the assembly work. The wisdom of training a new generation to take responsibility has become apparent, especially recently. The Serowe assembly now has the benefit of men who are seeking to forward the work of God and care for the flock. There are also younger sisters who keep busy behind the scenes.

None of us could have anticipated the events of 13th December 2018. Jim and Irene had travelled to Gaborone to pick up newly printed supplies of Bible lessons that had been outsourced to a company there. On their way home, Irene was driving their truck. It overturned and Irene was killed immediately, whereas Jim sustained only minor injuries. The gospel literature was scattered all over the road and verges. No other vehicle or stray animal was involved. We were all shocked and greatly saddened at this sudden accident and traumatic loss. The believers came together to support Jim and help arrange the funeral. It was a large gathering, with Jim's daughter Judy and son Crawford, his two sisters and other friends from the UK travelling to be there. Irene's body was laid to rest in the sandy ground of the village graveyard not far from their home.

Irene was dedicated, hardworking and meticulous in everything she did, with a real love for people. When she was busy and 'in full flight', the rest of us struggled to keep up. Earlier in 2018, the Botswana government had honoured her and Jim with the Presidential Order of Merit in recognition of their contribution to the development of the nation for 50 years.

Jim and Irene Legge

Jim bravely continued alone in Serowe. The elders were able to keep the assembly work going and the sisters cared for Jim in a practical way, providing meals, doing his shopping, and tending to many other tasks. About a year later, Jim took ill and was admitted to hospital in Francistown. Judy and Crawford came urgently to visit him and as a family they decided that he should return with them to the UK in December 2019. Shortly after moving into a retirement care home in Fife, Jim succumbed to Covid-19 and died on 24th April 2020. His elder sister, Margaret, who was also a resident in the home, passed away a few days later. They were buried together in Cowdenbeath. All of us in Botswana keenly feel the loss of Jim and Irene. We remain thankful for the sterling example of their devoted lives and service – "whose faith follow" (Hebrews 13.7) – and as we loved to sing at the end of the Serowe conference, 'Re tlaa rakana' (Till we meet again).

Continued Progress

Since Jim's death, the believers in the Serowe assembly have faithfully continued to serve the Lord. There was concern about the correspondence and literature work, and whether or not this would be maintained. The Lord challenged the office staff and they shared the conviction that they should seek to continue the work, as was Jim's desire, looking to the Lord to provide for their needs. For many years there has been the hope that local brethren and sisters in Botswana would one day be prepared to launch out in faith. We have been cheered to see this take place, even at a time of loss and readjustment.

The assemblies in Botswana now feel a burden and responsibility to support these and other local workers. Local brethren have established a fund to facilitate this. We continue to pray that this exercise will prosper and that the Lord will be honoured in it all.

Office Staff

Chapter 7

GABORONE

Gaborone is the capital city of Botswana with a population of over 250,000 people; this represents 10% of the total population of the country. Almost half of the nation lives within a radius of 60 miles from the capital. The city takes its name from Kgosi Gaborone, paramount chief of the Batlokwa tribe who live in the nearby village of Tlokweng. The Bechuanaland Protectorate had been administered from Mafikeng, but a newly independent nation needed a new capital. Gaberones, as it was known then, was only a small government camp before independence; it would soon become one of the fastest-growing cities in the world. Urban life brings many challenges but also presents unique opportunities for evangelism.

The First Believers

When Kgosi and Dorcas Mompati moved to Gaborone as government doctors, their home became a centre for the small group of believers they found there. Five others gathered with them: an older Indian couple, Mr and Mrs P. J. Thomas, originally from Kerala, two Zimbabwean nurses, and a local girl, Agnes Medupe (sister of Mavis), who was a student nurse. They met to remember the Lord and also to study His Word together.

Jim and Irene visited Gaborone from time to time to encourage the small band of Christians. After we arrived in Serowe in 1982, we were able to join them on these trips and share the driving; the 400-mile round trip was completed in one day, setting off at dawn and arriving home around midnight or later. Kgosi and Dorcas were transferred to South Africa for further studies and the two Zimbabwean ladies returned to their home country. The remaining three believers were not able to meet regularly.

After spending two valuable years in Serowe, learning the language, culture, and much else besides, Hazel and I were exercised about moving to the capital to try and help maintain the small testimony. We prayed about it and consulted with Jim and Irene and our home assembly in Dundonald. They all supported us in every way.

Officials at the Ministry of Health interviewed me regarding a transfer: 'What exactly are you? Are you a missionary or are you a doctor?' I was able to explain that I was willing to offer part-time medical help as a volunteer, but I wished also to spend time in evangelism. The final agreement was that I would work part-time, five mornings a week, and visit two separate clinics in and around the capital each morning. We were promptly offered a fully furnished government house to rent.

On the day we moved, Jim and Irene helped transport our bits and pieces. We did not have much furniture of our own; however, we had acquired a battered but perfectly usable piano. Jim's next-door neighbours had put it up for sale when their children declared their preference for a colour television set instead. Before leaving us, Jim gave me the best advice I could ever have heard: 'Clark, when you begin working in Gaborone, it will be like starting afresh. Start as you mean to go on.'

An Unpromising Start

Our burden was to reach out with the gospel in the language of the people. Keeping in mind Jim's advice, during the first week I visited all of the homes in our street, introducing ourselves, and inviting the neighbours to a gospel meeting in our home. Our African neighbours were polite and welcoming; a number seemed grateful for the invitation and gave us hope that they might come.

On that first Thursday evening, we put our two children to bed, arranged a few chairs and hymnbooks in the small living room, and waited for the crowd to pour in. We had a long wait, as Hazel and I looked at the clock and we looked at each other. It became clear that no one was coming to our first gospel meeting in Gaborone. I mentioned to her that I had prepared a Setswana gospel message on Romans chapter one; instead, we would have a ministry meeting in English on the same chapter. After singing a hymn and praying, I stood to minister to my wife.

We were disappointed and felt small and weak. Perhaps that was exactly what God had intended because we began to pray as we had never prayed before. We realised that if there was going to be blessing in Gaborone, God would have to work. Also, we found comfort in the Scriptures, especially the Lord's words to Paul as he arrived in Corinth: "Be not afraid, but speak, and hold not thy peace: for I am with thee, and no man shall set on thee to hurt thee: *for I have much people in this city*" (Acts 18.9-10).

I began to visit the low-cost area nearby where there seemed to be a more favourable response. Personal contacts were built up slowly over time and confidence was gained. Looking back now, we are so glad of those lessons we had to begin learning, lessons of dependence upon God. We would have been much the poorer had we thought the whole matter was easy and depended upon our abilities.

Growing Opportunities

We had no such attendance problems when we organised the first Sunday School in our garden. Long before the time, a crowd of about 30 local boys and girls were waiting excitedly outside our gate. As the weeks passed, the number increased rapidly until 150 children from the surrounding district were attending. Hazel would take the small ones inside to the living room; I would remain outside with the older ones in a shaded area in the garden. It was a 'garden' in name only – a patch of sandy ground with not a blade of grass or a flower to be seen.

The First Sunday School

There were other opportunities to present the gospel. It was then the custom in the government clinics that a short prayer and singing of a hymn would commence the day's work. When invited to participate, I would open the Scriptures and comment on the reading. Access was also granted to visit the prison complex in Gaborone to preach to men and women on separate days.

Life was busy with medical work in the morning, afternoon visitation and several evening meetings for gospel preaching and Bible teaching in our home. Our children attended a local pre-school where they were the only Europeans. Their best friends were the Batswana children in our street. They soon became fluent in the language, speaking with the right intonation in a way that their parents envied. While we continued to struggle with difficult grammatical constructions, Heather and Andrew rattled them off perfectly with ease.

Every Sunday morning, the Lord's Day, we sat down with our three Christian friends who had been part of the first small assembly group to remember the Lord in the breaking of bread and drinking of the cup. In the evening we studied the Scriptures together. Even though we were small in number, the presence of the Lord made it sweet. Had He not said, "For where two or three are gathered together in my name, there am I in the midst of them" (Matthew 18.20)? It was true, He was there, even in our home.

Mr and Mrs Thomas would bring their daughter, Irene, who was eventually saved, baptised and added to the assembly. After qualifying as a nurse, Agnes stayed with us for a time. Today, she is married with grandchildren. She and her husband, Modisa Motswaledi, with their daughter and son-in-law are faithful members of the assembly.

For almost two years we saw no fruit in terms of anyone trusting Christ. And yet, the Lord encouraged us to keep going. Things that others might have considered to be small or inconsequential, were to us evidence of the Lord's presence with us. Perhaps a neighbour would come for the first time, or a young person would ask a good question about the Bible; we would thank the Lord for these signs of interest.

The Firstfruit in Blessing

In the Lord's own time and in His own way, the blessing came. In October of 1985, a male prisoner called Oitlogetse Rantaung professed faith in Christ. He was serving a sentence of five years for having committed a serious crime. In prison, he faithfully attended the gospel meeting every week. When he trusted Christ, the prison officers were sceptical and informed me: 'They often say they have been saved. They are hoping that their sentence will be reduced or that we will treat them more favourably. It will never last.' As I write, over thirty-five years later, whatever Oitlogetse got in prison has lasted until today. He is one of my closest friends and now a respected elder in the Gaborone assembly.

After being released, this young man proved the reality of salvation. He refused to take part in any traditional family ceremonies related to his release. When he went for job interviews, he told the truth about his past, so that for many months he was without work. He had learned carpentry in prison and put this to good use by making wooden benches for our Sunday School. He also finely crafted a small table we still use regularly; on it each week are placed bread and wine as we remember our Lord.

Eventually, Oitlogetse was given the most junior post in a financial firm. His desk was just at the door as you entered. Within a few years, he had become the branch manager with his personal office upstairs. When he built his first home in Gaborone, he held a small opening ceremony with prayer and thanksgiving to God, followed by a week of gospel meetings for his friends and neighbours. This contrasted with the common practice of involving a traditional doctor to provide protection for a new house. He maintained his spiritual priorities and after being baptised he became a valuable asset to the assembly.

Oitlogetse and Nkamo Rantaung

We had already held our first baptism, using a portable swimming pool in the garden of a kind Christian friend. A young schoolboy had also been saved towards the end of 1985. He was baptised along with Irene Thomas. After the new hall was built, all subsequent baptisms took place there.

Gaborone Gospel Hall

After applying for a church plot, we were eventually offered a small plot not far from our home in the north of Gaborone. We were given little choice in the matter. Established denominations often seemed to be allocated large corner sites, but we did not complain, taking this provision as from the Lord. The plot itself was marked as state land and had to be purchased. It was a considerable amount of money that we did not have at that time, but like so many others who have told the Lord alone about their needs, we proved His faithfulness. Unexpectedly, a gift came through from our friends, George and Ena Wiseman, formerly of Angola and Zimbabwe, and this enabled us to proceed. A Christian architect from the assembly in Pretoria, South Africa, drew up plans for a hall. On our first week to use the new hall, the whole Sunday School walked from our garden to the hall, singing as we went. In July of 1987, the official opening was marked by a weekend conference of thanksgiving and Bible teaching.

The work grew slowly in Gaborone, but some years were especially fruitful, and many were saved. A Sunday School child would be saved, bring the mother to the gospel meeting and she would be saved. (There was not always a father in the picture.) The mother's salvation meant that there was now a new Christian family, shining as a bright testimony in the district. This happened time and again.

While most new believers were young folk, an elderly widow started to attend. We called her simply *Nkuku* ('Granny'). She would walk round from the nearby low-cost area where she stayed with her only daughter who had many children. Somehow, they would all find a space to sleep in the small, two-bedroomed house. She began to be troubled about her soul. When she was a young woman, she had dreamt about the Lord Jesus Christ. Her church minister assured her that she was now ready for heaven. This had been her anchor for many years. We had to show her, gently but firmly, that simply having a dream could never be enough. Finally, one day in 1987, she sat on our sofa and through understanding the truth of John 1.12, she received Christ. She was a stalwart believer in the assembly all of her remaining days until the Lord called her home in 2000 at 91 years of age.

Nkuku

Nkuku had very few personal possessions. From time to time Hazel would visit her at home and give her a gift of warm clothing, especially before winter. The next week she would attend the meetings and Hazel would ask, 'Nkuku, where's your scarf? Where's your cardigan?' Usually, the reply came back that the grandchildren had taken them and claimed them as their own. We can never forget the day she shuffled round from her home to visit us. She wore a headscarf as is common here among older women in Botswana. That day, she sat down and began to undo a knot in her scarf to reveal two little coins, our equivalent of two pennies: 'These are for the children, Sethunya and Kgosietsile.' We were so touched by this sacrificial gift; it reminded us of another poor widow whose selfless generosity brought pleasure to the Lord (Mark 12.42-44).

Blessing in the Home

Our home became a port-of-call for many believers from other areas of Botswana. They might come down for a few days or even stay for a longer time. As mentioned, Agnes lived with us after completing her training as a nurse. We had a small outside apartment, separate from the main house. This would be where Joy Griffiths would make her home for several years after her arrival in 1990. Later, when Heather Beggs joined us, she lived in a small caravan in the back garden. This was the nearest we ever came to resemble a mission station!

Joy and Friends

Joy Griffiths had been jointly commended from Marine Hall (Eastbourne), Toftwood (Norfolk) and Waterlooville (Hampshire) in 1990. She had first heard of the work in Botswana through listening to a recording of the London Missionary Meetings in 1981. She visited us in 1988 but was left wondering how a single woman could cope in Botswana. On returning to the UK, the Lord graciously used a message from the late Ray Fenn of Bolivia to confirm His call to Joy and to give her peace and assurance. She has been a faithful friend and co-worker for many years. She teaches children in Sunday School classes and in a government school; she also encourages the ladies of the assembly, both young and old, in many different ways. She is kind to everyone she meets. She has had opportunities through hospital visitation and tract distribution to witness for Christ and regularly has opened her home for special gospel meetings, inviting her neighbours and many other contacts to attend as the brethren preached each night.

Heather Beggs from Dromore, Northern Ireland, came to Botswana in 1992. She was quick to gain a working knowledge of Setswana. Being medically qualified, she became involved in the government home-based care scheme for the many sick patients we had to deal with at that time. After moving to Mochudi, her home was a convenient location for gospel outreach in the village. Heather returned to the UK in 1995 and after marrying Crawford Brown, they have been serving the Lord together in Brazil.

When other believers visited, our children would willingly give up their beds. They never complained about this; it added excitement to their routine. A young Christian once stayed with us for two weeks. Years later, she wrote to tell us that this had been her first time in a Christian home. Her own home had been marked by parental strife and abuse. She explained that she used to look carefully at my wife every morning, checking for bruises or other signs of injury. She concluded that she was probably beaten by her husband at night when everyone else was asleep. Only slowly did she realise that Christian homes were different.

At times there were those who sought refuge in our home. A female prisoner had professed faith in Christ. After her release, one night her husband tried to kill her using a knife; she arrived at our gate in desperation. She later fled to her home village where we were able to visit her until we lost touch with her. On another occasion, during a time of disturbance and rioting in the city, the Christian students at the university sheltered with us. The army had entered the campus looking for troublemakers and the innocent were in danger of getting caught in the middle.

There were so many visitors in those days that we find it hard to remember all of their names. Several were like 'angels' in the blessing that they brought and the fragrance of Christ they left behind. The late Tommy Thompson of Alaska visited twice. He was able to encourage us in a special way: sizing up our homelife, he advised us to make sure that we reserved a little time in the busy week to spend with our children. Friday afternoon worked best for us. Also, in the beginning when we had little fellowship, Jack Strahan of Northern Ireland paid us a brief visit. We will never forget the effect of those few days in which he lifted our spirits and ministered Christ to us.

Our home became the birthplace of many souls, including our own little boy who had been anxious to be saved. One night his sister opened her Setswana Bible to read a few verses to him. Later that evening, as we joined in the discussion, he trusted Christ as his Saviour. Andrew's best friend who lived next door was saved. Heather's best friend, Dondo, who lived across the street was also saved, and yet another friend next door to her. In this way Heather and Andrew made contacts and opened many other doors that the Lord blessed. Several members of a Ugandan family who lived at the end of the street trusted Christ. In the low-cost area nearby, not only was Nkuku saved, but also three other young women and a schoolboy. And so, God blessed beyond our expectations.

Gaborone West

Most of the initial development in Gaborone had occurred to the east of the main railway line. In the years of rapid city expansion, the bush area to the west began to be cleared and prepared for further development. Denis Gilpin of Jersey, UK, paid us an appreciated visit and one day, as we drove around the empty plots on the west side of the city, he suggested we might consider expanding the work to the new area.

The story of how we first applied but then had to wait for 10 years before we acquired a plot could fill a book. When it seemed that all our efforts were in vain, the Lord in a marvelous way enabled us to obtain a plot on which Gaborone West Gospel Hall was constructed. It was designed to be low maintenance and also to provide adequate cooking facilities for conferences and other larger gatherings. We had an opening conference in 2001 with Alec Legge and Jack Hay and helping us. Notably, on that occasion we also learned a beautiful Scottish tune to one of our favourite hymns. It is still our tune of choice for that hymn.

At first, the hall was one of the few buildings in the new area. The situation soon changed with many homes springing up around it. What was even more encouraging was that local people, notably four adult women, heard the gospel and were saved. They are all now in assembly fellowship. We continue to use it as an outreach venue.

Subsequent Growth

While the Gaborone assembly has grown numerically, our main concern is for spiritual growth and maturity in the lives of the believers. It is always a joy when new believers begin to have a concern for others and become soul-winners and devoted servants in the assembly. We have benefitted too from the help of Zambian and Indian believers in fellowship. For many years it has been an honour to share the burden of shepherding with three godly local brethren. I have learnt so many valuable lessons from Oitlogetse, Letsibogo and Donald. We are aware of the many changes and challenges all around us in Gaborone but take heart in trusting an unchanging God.

Chapter 8

FRANCISTOWN

Francistown is Botswana's second-largest city with a population of over 100,000 people. It is located in the north-east of the country, about 270 miles from Gaborone, near the confluence of several rivers. Its history is linked with the discovery of gold and other minerals in the area, and the city is named after Daniel Francis, an English prospector from Liverpool. The town was founded in 1897, being conveniently situated near the Monarch gold mine. It grew rapidly and before independence was Botswana's main commercial centre, being close to the border with Rhodesia (now Zimbabwe). It was declared to be a city in 1997 and it remains an important transport and business hub.

A significant percentage of the population of Francistown and the surrounding area are people belonging to the Kalanga tribe. They have their own language and culture, and their history is intertwined with that of the people of Matebeleland in southern Zimbabwe. The Bible has been translated into Kalanga. In Francistown there are also large numbers of Zimbabwean immigrants in the city, seeking employment.

Early Days

Ian and Rebecca Rees came to Botswana in 1984 (see Chapter

City Skyline

6). Ian's parents, Norman and Iris Rees, had served the Lord in Zambia from 1954-1971, and so Ian was no stranger to Africa. He had attended the University of Aberystwyth where he came to know and appreciate the presence of the late John Heading in the small local assembly there.

They arrived with their infant son, Adam, and spent the first two years in the village of Serowe, engaging in language study and helping in the assembly, before moving to Francistown in 1985. At that time there was no assembly and no established evangelical work in the town. They began holding gospel meetings in their home. On Thursday evenings, Ian preached consecutively from the Old Testament, and on Sunday mornings he preached from the New Testament. It was during those early years that they made contact with a young man, Peter Marewa, who trusted Christ, was baptised, and received into fellowship. He would later transfer to Selebi-Phikwe. Mavis Medupe was based in Francistown at that time and training to be a midwife. She was instrumental in bringing a 12-year-old girl to hear the gospel, and so Ontiretse Boranabi ('Onty') was saved in 1990. Onty has happy memories of travelling with other Francistown believers to Nata to support the Mbangiwas at their annual Sunday School prizegiving.

Ian was interested in providing Christian literature and he opened a bookshop in the town, calling it *'Peo e e Tlhokegang'* (Precious Seed Bookroom). Peter Marewa helped in running the shop. A Ghanaian man, Charles Van Dyk, came looking for Bible study material and subsequently he came to hear the gospel in the Rees's home. He and Peter were the first two believers baptised in Francistown, in a neighbour's swimming pool. Charles's wife, Arabah, subsequently trusted Christ, was baptised and added to the assembly. They would later return to Ghana where they are still active in Christian witness. Ian translated *Ultimate Questions* into Setswana and also some hymns into the language. These were included in a bilingual hymnbook.

Kgosi and Dorcas Mompati moved to Francistown in 1988. Their medical studies had taken them from Botswana to Uganda and then Kenya. After that, there were spells of further training in South Africa and an extended stay in Scotland. It was their joy to be part of the Cowdenbeath assembly of Christians which was Jim and Irene's home assembly. Their son, Daniel, was born in the UK. Kgosi worked in many of the hospitals in the area and later obtained his higher medical qualification from the Royal College of Physicians in Edinburgh.

In Francistown, they formed part of the small group of eight believers who met together to break bread as a new assembly on 12th June of that year. In the following years, other believers including several Zambians were added to the company of believers. Ivan and Lenyora Mbangiwa, early converts from Serowe days, would visit as they were able. Ivan was appointed as the headmaster in government school some two hours away in a place called Nata. After retirement, they maintained a home in the Francistown area. Presently, Kgosi and Ivan are elders in the Francistown assembly.

Kgosi worked as a physician in the Jubilee Hospital in Francistown. He recalls that 1988 was a year of heavy rains and flooding when many people died of malaria. He had been approached by the mining company in Selebi-Phikwe with the offer of a lucrative medical post there. This was the first of several attractive offers that would have taken him away to another location, but the Lord showed him clearly that he and his family should remain in Francistown. He and his wife continue in medical practice in the city.

Tsholofelo Hall

Subsequently, application was made to the Town Council to request a suitable plot for a church building. A spacious plot was duly granted, and a large hall was constructed, designed with a central courtyard and baptistry and surrounding blocks of

Tsholofelo Hall

classrooms. Not only was the council site granted without charge, but also a Christian architect from Zimbabwe offered his services freely. Tsholofelo (Hope) Hall was opened with a Bible conference.

The Francistown Sunday School had begun initially under the shade of a large tree in a township area just opposite the Rees's home. The numbers grew and the children transferred to a shaded area in the garden. The Sunday School would eventually grow to about 200 children and this included a number of deaf children who came from a nearby special school. Rebecca, and later other believers, learned sign language so that they could communicate the love of God to these children.

A work commenced with the homeless children in the town. Many of these children spent their day begging; sometimes the proceeds were spent on sniffing glue rather than eating food. They were offered a mid-day meal outside the bookshop but eventually, a vacant building in the town was provided where a 'school' was set up to teach them Bible stories and crafts. Good attenders were rewarded with clothing. The business community was generous in supporting this work.

Ian visited other assemblies from time to time, such as Selebi-Phikwe within Botswana, another small assembly in Bulawayo, Zimbabwe, and believers in Livingstone, Zambia. One Zambian believer, Ben Chandalala, discovered that he had been born only five days before Ian in the same mission hospital in Zaire. Several Zambian believers went on to form the nucleus of an English-speaking assembly in Livingstone which was subsequently assisted by David McAllister. Visits were also made to Maun to encourage Dan Nguluka, and later Sid and Karen Halsband. In 1997, after seeing the establishment of the assembly in

Francistown, Ian and Rebecca decided to return to the UK. They continued to serve the Lord in the Bath area and more recently in Tenby in Wales.

Reinforcements

Jane Motlaleselelo (née Wood) from Cardiff spent five years in Francistown, from 1989-1994. After language study, she was able to help Ian and Rebecca with work amongst the children. Thereafter, she had opportunities to teach scripture in three local schools as well as visiting the children's ward in the local hospital. Following her marriage to a local brother, Selelo Motlaleselelo, the government transferred Selelo to Maun. Their next eight years were spent there, and Jane became a mother to twins, Tshegofatso and Tsholofelo (Grace and Hope). As is the Setswana custom, she became known as MmaTshegofatso. Subsequently, two other daughters would be added to the family.

Jane's husband received another transfer, taking the family to the town of Kasane. There was no assembly there, but Jane was exercised to do a work among the children using her own home. Five years later, the family moved back 'home' to Francistown. Jane continues to help in children's work, not only in the area of the Gospel Hall but also in outlying areas. She is burdened about the school-leavers as well as the young believers, and she has helped to organise special times of teaching for them. On occasions she has been able to support Mavis Medupe in Shoshong with her group of young folk and also help the Raggetts with literature distribution in the Palapye area.

John and Margaret Rutter came to Francistown from Bath in 1994. As well as engaging in language study, John worked in the bookshop and assisted with the street children. He and Margaret opened their home for gospel meetings. Their daughters, Naomi and

Sunday School Class

Jessica, attended school in Francistown. At the beginning of 1997, the Rutters were approached by the two elders from Selebi-Phikwe and invited to assist the small assembly here. Albert Horan from Northern Ireland had come to the end of his teaching contract and was due to return to his homeland. The other brother, Martin Solomoni, had already been transferred to Francistown. The Rutters felt that they should move to Selebi-Phikwe and help to keep the work going. They would remain there until returning to England in 2006 for their childrens' education.

John Bandy first visited Botswana in 1998 and assisted in practical work. In keeping with his previous work experience, he was able to carry out renovations to the Francistown assembly hall. It was during this time that he and Ontiretse (mentioned above) befriended one another. Two years later, John was commended by the Hanslope assembly in England and after returning to Botswana, he married Onty in 2000. Together John and Onty became involved in all aspects of the assembly work. Onty was John's in-house language teacher.

They presently live in Tati Siding, 10 miles south of Francistown. Since 2012, John has been able to visit primary schools in Francistown, Tonota village, Tati Siding and other villages where he takes their morning assemblies. A Sunday School in their own home has been blessed in salvation with two older boys being saved, baptised, and added to the assembly. Several others have been saved and baptised.

The Bandys are grateful for household salvation with their three children, Rejoice, Thomas and James, having professed faith in Christ. Rejoice is now part of the assembly. Another young relative, Gaone, also stayed with them for some years and got saved. Her mother was Onty's cousin. John continues his involvement in literature work and at conference times he sets up a book table where Bibles and study books in both Setswana and English are readily available. In more recent years he assisted the Serowe assembly to construct a large open-roofed area beside the hall. This provides shade and shelter from the elements and during conference times it has proved invaluable.

Baptism

Francistown also had the help of David and Helen McKillen from Kells in Northern Ireland. Initially they had been interested in serving the Lord in Zambia but were directed to Francistown after they both visited Botswana in 2002. They arrived with their two youngest children in 2005. They began to study Setswana and adapt to their new surroundings. They were encouraged when the woman who worked in their home, a Zimbabwean lady called Irene, trusted the Lord. When a problem arose with her immigration papers, she spent a few days in prison, but she was sustained in her faith. David made visits to the believers in Maun as well as other places in neighbouring countries such as Zambia, Namibia, and Zimbabwe.

Locally there arose an opportunity to visit regularly the 'Immigrant' Prison outside Francistown. Despite initial obstacles, official permission was also granted to visit the large refugee camp at Dukwi, over 60 miles from Francistown. At that time there were around 30,000 residents. David and John shared in this work of gospel preaching, Bible teaching, and conducting a large Sunday School. Items for attendance prizes were sent in a container by the believers in Kells, Northern Ireland; these were widely distributed to the many nationalities in the camp.

An English teaching magazine was commenced known as the *African Believer's Magazine*. This magazine and other items such as calendars and tracts were printed in Cape Town. David travelled to collect these and then distribute them widely. While in Cape Town, he was able to preach the gospel with Rodney Brown. David and Helen began to feel that it would be more convenient to centre their labours in South Africa and so, with the blessing of their home assembly in Kells and the Francistown believers, they relocated to Cape Town in 2009. Since their return to Northern

Ireland in 2013 on account of Helen falling ill, they have continued to keep in touch with believers in South Africa and Botswana.

The Work at Present

In earlier years there were expatriate believers from Zambia in the Francistown assembly where their contribution to all aspects of assembly life was valued. With the gradual changes in government policy, their conditions of employment altered and became less favourable. Most of them have returned to their home country or moved overseas.

Regular gospel efforts continue using the hall as the venue. Just as in other places in Botswana, the brethren report that it is becoming more difficult to interest people to come and hear the word of God. Nevertheless, they continue to sow the seed through literature distribution and to proclaim the truth of the gospel to children and adults alike.

At the end of September, the two days of the Independence holiday fluctuate form year to year, but when they are close to a weekend the assembly has hosted a three-day Bible conference. There is then enough time for believers from afar to travel to and from the conference. At their last conference in 2019, historical reports were given from all over Botswana telling of the progress of the work over the past 50 years. Jim Legge was able to take part, but none of us thought that this would be the last occasion he would speak in public in Francistown. A special celebratory cake was baked, iced with our national colours, and Jim performed the necessary surgery on it before we all enjoyed it.

Chapter 9

SELEBI-PHIKWE

The town of Selebi-Phikwe, 62 miles south-east of Francistown, grew rapidly around a copper-nickel mine which was established in 1974. The population soon rose to 50,000. The government of Botswana held a 15 per cent share in the BCL company (Bamangwato Concessions Ltd.). The ore was extracted from shafts in deep, opencast mines and transported by rail beyond Botswana's borders. The construction of the Letsibogo Dam nearby and the subsequent construction of the coal-fired Morupule power station outside Palapye were vital components of the venture. The government also tried to diversify the economy of the town by attracting textile companies to set up their operations in the town. Financial assistance was offered to outside investors but the realities of the global economy, particularly in the face of fierce competition from Asian exporters, soon began to bite. Few if any of the original clothing companies remain.

The global economic meltdown also affected the demand for mineral ore and the mine began to run at a loss. Various costly interventions by the government over several years, amounting to nearly 5 billion Pula (£340 million), held off closure until the inevitable decision was made in 2016 to terminate mining operations. Around 5,000 people were suddenly made redundant.

The negative impact on the life of the small town also has had repercussions for the promising gospel and assembly work that had begun there several decades earlier.

Jim and Irene Legge visited the town in 1970 and Jim reported afterwards: 'We are looking to the Lord to give us wisdom whether we ought to get a piece of land with the hope of doing work there later on.' It would be 20 years later that the work would begin there in earnest with the arrival of a young Zambian couple and their family.

Help from Zambia

Levi and Abigail Zulu arrived in Gaborone on a hot October afternoon in 1989 with their two young sons, Isaac and Daniel. A few months later Abigail gave birth to their daughter, Tamara, in the local hospital. Levi had come to work as a civil engineer. The day after their arrival they made contact with the Gaborone assembly believers and Levi joined them on a visit to the diamond mining town of Jwaneng, 100 miles away, to encourage Mavis Medupe who was working as a nurse in the mine hospital. Levi was impressed as he listened to one of the Gaborone brethren, Oitlogetse Rantaung, speaking in Mavis's home and relating the story of his conversion. The two men became firm friends.

Levi and Abigail gave themselves wholeheartedly to the assembly and its activities, but they found the language strange and very different from the two Zambian languages they knew already. Soon they would become keen students and have regular Setswana lessons with Clark Logan. These lessons began to bear fruit as they began communicating with local people. They were friendly and outgoing with anyone they met and proved to be a great asset to the assembly.

The Zulu Family

In his employment, Levi was transferred to Selebi-Phikwe in August of 1990 to be the chief engineer of an infrastructure development project. The believers of the Gaborone assembly were sorry to see the Zulus go. Soon after settling into a new home in the town, Levi was approached about helping a church group who were looking for a new pastor and thought he might be a good replacement. He politely declined, choosing rather to open his own home for the study of the Scriptures and preaching of the gospel, using his recently-acquired knowledge of Setswana. One of the first contacts Levi and Abigail had was the mother of a young man called Reuben Zilwa. She would come along with her family but despite efforts made to befriend her husband, he did not come. In due course, two elderly ladies also began attending with the children from their households as well as several young men.

Help from Northern Ireland

Around October of 1990, an Irish brother called Albert Horan together with his wife Shan came to Phikwe and joined the small group of believers there. Albert lectured at the local Technical Training Centre. They had a toddler called Sarah who became friends with Tamara, the Zulu's little daughter. (Levi fondly remembers how Tamara would call her friend 'Sewa', and Sarah would call her friend 'Tamawa'). As a single man, Albert had previously worked as a teacher in Zambia so he already had experience of working in Africa. The Zulus and Horans worked closely together and the meetings transferred to the Horan's home. Albert was tireless in using his van to collect people from distant areas, transporting them to the meetings and then taking them back home. When he and Shan returned to Northern Ireland in 1997, they left their vehicle for the use of the assembly work. Upon his retirement from teaching in 2018, Albert was suddenly called home to heaven.

Other assemblies offered what support they could give in terms of occasional visits to encourage the believers in Phikwe. Through consistent efforts using their homes, people began to trust in the Lord. Regular open-air work was conducted in the central shopping mall. New believers were taken to Francistown, the nearest assembly where they could be baptised. Levi and Abigail appreciated the fellowship of Kgosi and Dorcas Mompati of Francistown. The bonds of friendship that were established then have continued until the present day.

In mid-1991, a plot of ground in a western suburb of Phikwe was procured. Initially, a simple shelter of gumtree poles and netting was erected. The believers began to meet there on Lord's Day. The local area was visited and evangelised while contacts from the eastern side of the town in Botshabelo were maintained. The small assembly prayed concerning the construction of a hall and they were encouraged to see how the Lord provided resources, both from within Botswana and from overseas, to erect a building that suited their needs including Sunday School work. More local people began to attend and some were saved at that time. A young man, Koketso Buisanyang, had been saved through hearing the gospel in the village of Rasesa near Gaborone. He was posted north in the national service scheme for school-leavers (*Tirelo Setshaba*), and would travel to Phikwe to spend his weekends there. His help with gospel preaching and also translating for Albert or Levi was invaluable.

Levi and Abigail with their three children returned to their home country of Zambia in 1993. They met with an assembly of Christians in Lusaka where Levi maintained a bright testimony and helped to shepherd the flock. He became the director of a large engineering company and was also appointed as Zambia's honorary consul for Indonesia. When he was approached about this latter post, and knowing that Indonesia was predominantly Muslim, he made clear that he was a believer in Christ; this did not sway the appointments panel – they wanted *him*. The family passed through a deep trial when, in July of 2010, Abigail was involved in a fatal road accident and called home to heaven.

Help from England

In February of 1997, the elders of the Phikwe assembly, Albert Horan and Martin Solomoni, approached John and Margaret Rutter who were then working in Francistown. The elders asked the Rutters to consider coming to help as they both would soon be leaving the town. Subsequently, the Lord confirmed that Phikwe was to be the place where the Rutters would focus their labours. At that time there were about 12 believers in fellowship.

On Sunday mornings, John and Margaret taught two classes of children under a tree. This was followed by a gospel meeting and John records that for over nine years he preached through the book of Genesis, including teaching for any believers who would be present. The Breaking of Bread meeting would follow. On Wednesday and Sunday evenings there would be Bible teaching from the New Testament (Romans through to Jude). One of the sisters in fellowship started teaching young children in the Botshabelo area and this work developed until there were three separate classes held there. In the same area of town, John was able to have Bible studies in various homes, sometimes that of a believer and at other times the home of an unbeliever. He taught consecutively through the Gospel of Mark and the Acts of the Apostles. On Friday evenings, the Rutters would invite the young people to their home for Bible teaching and fellowship.

There were also opportunities to preach in the local prison. Initially, attendance for the prisoners was voluntary but a new governor made attendance compulsory. A prison chaplain helped to organise meetings with the prison officers. Twice a week John was also able to give a short message in a local clinic, before the day's work began.

Personal work involved many home visits and these yielded fruit in salvation. Margaret would often visit older women accompanied by one of the Christian ladies from the assembly. One woman they visited admitted to being heavily involved in witchcraft but after trusting Christ she threw away everything that was connected with her former way of life. She became seriously ill and not long after trusting Christ, she was called home to heaven. The assembly members conducted her funeral. A relative of this lady was subsequently saved and became a faithful member of the assembly, after giving up the running of a shebeen (an unlicensed drinking den). This had been her former source of income. Margaret also maintained contacts with several expatriate ladies with whom she would study the Scriptures.

Sunday School

During the Rutter's time in Botswana, their two daughters attended four different schools. There were safety concerns when they attended school in Bulawayo, Zimbabwe, so homeschooling was necessary for a period. This difficult situation prompted the Rutters to return to the UK in June of 2006 and hand over the care of the work to Bryan and Joanna Jenkins.

Help from Wales and Francistown

Bryan and Joanna had originally spent a period of missionary service in Zimbabwe, but they were in the UK when they became interested in helping the work at Phikwe. They came out with their daughter, Lauren Joy, in 2006 and took over from the Rutters.

Bryan applied himself to language learning and he and Joanna continued to assist the work in Phikwe for the next six years. In 2013, serious health issues affecting Joanna's parents necessitated their return to the UK. Joanna's father was called home in May of that same year. Bryan himself has been unwell in the last few years.

In the Lord's goodness, Peter Marewa and his wife, Bethildah, with their two children had moved to Phikwe in 2013 to take up employment at the BCL mine. They did not find it easy at first to assume the responsibility for the assembly. Some believers left the assembly, and this affected not only the general attendance but also the Sunday School work. Both Peter and Bethildah had demanding jobs – he was often 'on the road' away from home – and if they were delayed, the meeting was cancelled. They did their best to make adjustments and sacrifices for the sake of the assembly.

Selebi-Phikwe believers

This came to a head with the closure of the mine and the loss of their employment. Bethildah has been able to find occasional contract work but Peter has not been successful so far in this regard. Nevertheless, Peter is burdened to remain in Phikwe and help maintain the assembly work there. The whole life of the town of Phikwe has been affected as mentioned above. Peter reports that about ten new churches have sprung up in the area of the Gospel Hall; these are offering food and musical entertainment and, unsurprisingly, local people are attracted to attend.

Onkutule Mosupiemang is a pharmacy technician working in government service. He was transferred to Mmadinare village, not far from Phikwe. He is now married to Tshepho and they have a baby daughter. This couple has also been faithful in seeking to maintain the assembly work in Phikwe. They hope that they will not be transferred to another location that would take him away from the area. Mothusi Keitirile, a schoolteacher, and his wife have joined the small assembly more recently.

There are presently ten believers in fellowship. The Sunday School teaches about 60 young ones, two of whom were recently saved. Approaches have been made to visit two new primary schools in the area. Every year, Bibles are given to the community and to the school-leavers of Kopano Primary School. Many gospel tracts are also regularly distributed. The Christians in the assembly value prayer as they seek to continue reaching out with the gospel and living for Christ in Selebi-Phikwe.

Chapter 10

MAUN

Maun is the tourist centre of Botswana and is situated in the far north-west of the country. It is the gateway to the Okavango Delta and the Moremi Game Reserve with many tour and safari companies based there. From the local airport, private flights transport tourists to and from the more remote safari camps. Until the completion of the tarred roadway from Nata, Maun's remoteness gave it the character of a frontier town. The commonest form of transport seen in the town were mud-spattered 4x4 vehicles, essential for negotiating the rough bush roads. In recent years, the town has developed rapidly and now boasts modern shops and malls, hotels and services in common with other urban areas. The developing road network throughout Botswana has meant Maun is now more accessible.

Maun has been the capital of the Batawana tribe since 1915. Other smaller tribes are found in the area including those whose lives are closely intertwined with the waterways of the Delta. The Basubiya, Bayei, and Hambukushu are well known for their skills in fishing and basket weaving. Men from these tribes often find employment with safari companies because of their expertise at navigating the narrow channels of the Delta by poling the dug-out canoes known as *mekoro*.

Shakawe and Seronga

A Zambian brother, Dan Nguluka, had been commended to the grace of God for gospel work in 1983, serving the Lord in the Solwezi area of Zambia. He and his wife, Stella, began to be exercised about Botswana after hearing a report in 1988 of an open door for evangelism. They arrived in Botswana in 1991with their young family: their daughter, Luwi, was then two years of age and their son, Ntanga, was six weeks old.

Their first year was spent in Shakawe, over 200 miles north of Maun and near the border with the Caprivi Strip. Stella had a teaching post in the local secondary school. Dan and Stella began to learn Setswana and they were encouraged when a young woman called Polokelo trusted the Lord. The next year they moved to the village of Seronga where there seemed to be an even greater interest in hearing the Word of God. Every Sunday their home was a centre for evangelism as young people from the local secondary school and older people from the village gathered to hear the good news of the gospel.

A young man called Donald Moilwe was spending his national service year in Seronga. His own home was in the village of Mochudi, not far from Gaborone. He was a believer and showed a keen spiritual interest in both gospel work and Bible study. Dan and he spent many hours together discussing the Scriptures. Donald had been formerly linked with another church group, but his convictions were moulded and changed as he began to understand more clearly the teachings of the New Testament. In due course, he would leave his former church, but he did so in a respectful and gracious way. He first met with his pastor in Mochudi and opened the Scriptures with him. The pastor admitted that he was unable to answer Donald's questions or address his concerns. They parted ways amicably.

Dan and Donald worked closely together, and the Lord began to save several young men and women. When these new believers completed their basic secondary education in Seronga, most would transfer to Maun for further studies. They were able to make use of a classroom so that Dan could visit them each month for Bible teaching. They also invited their friends to come and hear the gospel. Occasionally, other believers from different assemblies – Francistown, Serowe, Gaborone – were able to make the long journey by road and boat to visit Seronga and help in the work there and also in Maun. In 1996 Dan and Stella relocated to Sehithwa before eventually settling in Maun.

Trials

Sid and Karen Halsband with their three small boys arrived in Botswana from Canada in November of 1991. After spending a week with the Logans, they moved into a rented house and set about furnishing it. Shortly thereafter they commenced language study with Clark as their teacher. While Sid learned Setswana, his language teacher learned much more from Sid – vehicle maintenance, carpentry, how to fix computers, how to make strong coffee, and many other useful skills.

At Easter 1992, Sid was asked to give a ministry message at the national Bible conference. This was a big responsibility because he recalls, 'I wished they had asked me to preach the gospel instead of ministry. I knew the gospel message and had experienced it. What could I give in ministry that I knew about?' About a month after the conference he fell ill with what seemed to be flu-like symptoms and a sinus infection. That particular year, many others were similarly affected by what we regarded as influenza and there were also other serious health challenges (see Chapter 17). Sid was about to have experiences that would deepen his knowledge of the Lord and His ways.

This illness laid him aside for two weeks but suddenly developed into complete paralysis from the waist down. After Clark visited him at home on the morning of 9th June, Sid was transferred to the local private hospital without delay. He was admitted to the intensive care unit and spent several days there. The attending physician was gravely concerned upon examining him; life-threatening diagnoses such as cerebral malaria or an intracranial bleed were considered. Sid's level of consciousness deteriorated, and an emergency airlift to Johannesburg was hastily arranged. We recall that particular night when the Gaborone airport, normally closed at night, was specially reopened for a single passenger, permitting the arrival and departure of the small medevac Learjet.

For two weeks Sid lay in the hospital in Johannesburg. Eventually, the diagnosis was made of tuberculous meningitis. Jim Legge accompanied Sid on a flight from South Africa back home to Canada; Irene Legge was able to fly later with Karen and the three boys. In his long rehabilitation in Canada, the doctors at first warned Sid that he would never walk again. Sid and Karen both had assurance and peace that it would be otherwise. Sid eventually walked out of the hospital.

A New Horizon

After about a year and a half of rehabilitation, they felt that the Lord would have them return to Botswana. During the extended period of therapy in Canada, the Lord was teaching Sid and Karen many valuable lessons that would help them both in their ministry. The prime lesson for Sid was learned from the book of Philippians. As Sid described it, the Lord was doing a work *in* him, whereas he had been focused on what the Lord might do *through* him. In November 1993, they returned to Gaborone and continued with their language lessons. They were exercised about moving further afield and Maun was the place that caught their interest. Crawford Allison and George Wiseman had briefly passed through what was then only a small village many years before.

An initial exploratory trip to Maun gave Sid a feel for the place. On that visit, he had arranged to meet with several local residents who were selling land. One man had a way with words: after asking an exorbitant price for the plot he was selling, he quickly reminded us with great eloquence that this was nothing compared to the value of a soul! Sid declined his offer.

When the Halsband family left Gaborone to relocate to Maun, they had no guarantee of a place to stay when they arrived there. They loaded their pick-up van and a hired trailer with their household furniture and belongings. Three other fully laden vans belonging to Joy Griffiths, Heather Beggs, and the Logans completed the 'caravan'. This was the expedition that set off on the long trip to Maun in July of 1994. After an overnight stop in Francistown, all of the travellers arrived safely in Maun the next afternoon.

Building the Temporary Structure

An Assembly Planted

After staying in temporary accommodation for a period, the Halsbands procured a plot of land and proceeded to build their new house. This caused a lot of interest in the neighbourhood and by the time they moved into the new accommodation, they already had a familiar audience of young people and adults who began to attend gospel meetings and Sunday School classes under the trees in their garden.

They first broke bread as an assembly in their home on 23rd April 1995. In the company were two young women who had been saved earlier in Maun as well as Selelo Motlalelselelo and his wife, Jane (née Wood). A temporary thatched building with reed walls was erected in their garden. After several years, the assembly was able to buy a large plot nearby and the Lord provided all that was required for the erection of a spacious modern building. Sid and Dan did much of the planning and organising themselves. They hosted an opening Easter conference in 2008 and believers from all over Botswana attended.

Sunday School Transport

On several occasions, Sid and Karen also organised for a group of young men and women to visit from North America. This exposed them to missionary life in Africa and although limited by being unable to speak Setswana, they could help in various gospel activities during their stay.

Sid's physical condition was slowly but steadily deteriorating. After much prayer and concern, they moved to Cape Town in 2011 to be near the necessary medical facilities. Just before leaving Maun, they rejoiced to see a young man and woman, Dinyando and Thato Romai, united in marriage. They were the fruit of the Sunday School work and the brother is now an elder in the assembly. After some years in Cape Town, Sid and Karen were sad to leave Africa and relocate to Canada and the USA. They keep in regular touch with their friends in Botswana.

Although Sid is now permanently in a wheelchair, he writes: 'To be called of the Lord to serve Him on the foreign mission field is a tremendous honour and yet very challenging. It is a

The Maun Assembly

time to learn more of one's own shortcomings and failures, and to experience the grace and sustaining power of God. Had we another life to give in service to the Lord, we would do it again.'

Reinforcements

Preceding the Halsband's departure from Maun, Franklin and Jenny McIlroy relocated to Maun from Serowe in August 2010. Franklin joined Dan in continuing the gospel outreach. There were opportunities for open-air work and tract distribution in the town. The familiar 'Two Roads Chart' in Setswana was often used. Good contacts were made with people who showed an interest to hear more. Gospel calendars were also widely distributed.

Franklin had the liberty to visit the local prison and preach the gospel there. Every few weeks he was able to visit the police station and preach to 60-70 officers. Tent meetings were convened on several occasions. They held a children's meeting first in the afternoon and then the adults came later in the evening. Franklin relates that in their preaching they formed the habit of giving a summary of the whole message at the very end for those who arrived late and had missed the beginning. This also meant that those who arrived early had a double portion!

As in Serowe, Franklin and Jenny kept an open home for the believers, especially for the younger ones who needed regular Christian fellowship and good company. Franklin also continued to assist in the container work, liaising with his home assembly of Kells in Northern Ireland. Every year a container arrived, packed with Bibles and useful Sunday School materials that many believers had so generously donated. These would include clothing, toiletries, stationery, small toys and novelty items. These were used all over Botswana for the annual Sunday

School prize distribution in the different areas. For children unaccustomed to receiving such gifts, the day was eagerly awaited – a special day indeed. Franklin, Jenny and family returned to the UK in 2011.

Unloading the Container

The work continues in Maun. Dan Nguluka remains there even though his family situation has altered in that his wife no longer has employment in Botswana. From time to time believers are sent to Maun in government service so it is always a blessing for them to have a local assembly nearby. As with all of the assemblies in Botswana, the local believers in Maun value prayer, not only that the work might be preserved, but also that it might prosper.

Chapter 11

PALAPYE

Palapye is a rapidly growing town located on the main north-south road and rail routes between Gaborone and Francistown. For thirteen years (1889-1902), it was the capital of the Bamangwato tribe after Chief Khama III moved his people there from Shoshong. He would later relocate to Serowe, some 28 miles to the west. Between 1891 and 1894, a large LMS (London Missionary Society) church was constructed using burnt brick. The ruins are still visible in the area now known as Old Palapye. Chief Khama was said to have donated 3,000 Pounds to the project.

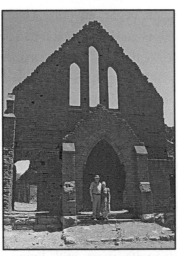

Ruins of the LMS Church

Nearby is the Morupule coal mine which feeds the two adjacent power stations, the country's main domestic source of electricity. The first phase in the construction of a new university on the outskirts of the town was completed in 2012. It is known as BIUST (Botswana International University of Science and Technology).

The main road runs north-south through the town and with the building of new fast-food outlets, filling stations and shopping malls, it provides a convenient stopping place for travellers. The large modern bus station is nearby. Goods from overseas addressed to Serowe used to arrive by rail at Palapye railway station, then they were transported by road to Serowe on a rough gravel and sand track. After a long day's journey heading back home, travellers to Serowe turned westwards at Palapye to face the full glare of the setting sun.

Early Opportunities

Over the years, occasional visits were made to Palapye for gospel preaching but no regular work was established until Colin and Christine Raggett began an outreach there in 1997. Their exercise regarding Botswana had developed gradually until they were both convinced of the Lord leading them to serve Him there. For 11 years, 1992-2003, they were in fellowship in Serowe and fully involved in the assembly activities. They applied themselves to language study, and the input of both Jim Legge and Topo Moleele meant that they and their three children became fluent in Setswana. Colin remembers Jim telling them on their first meeting back in 1990, 'If you don't both become fluent in the language, you'll not last in Botswana.' They took these words to heart and made language learning a priority.

In 1997, the Raggetts were still living in Serowe when

opportunities developed for a Sunday School work in Palapye in two locations. Colin recalls that 'the interest among the children was encouraging but we were very conscious that they knew nothing about the gospel, having been brought up under the superstition of witchcraft and traditional beliefs. We had to start with the basics.' A brother and sister from Serowe, Basaakane and Peggy Ogotseng, were living and working in Palapye at that time. They opened their home for the preaching of the gospel.

A regular bookstall was commenced in the main shopping area in Palapye and many people were contacted in this way. Good conversations were had with local people; some bought Setswana or English Bibles and most accepted gospel tracts. Due to redevelopment in the area, the location became unsuitable, but it served its purpose well at the time.

Soon there were other opportunities to present the gospel, especially in various home yards. Initially, there were four different locations for regular preaching and the Lord began to move in blessing with salvation. This brought much encouragement. Such meetings continued in Palapye, especially during the dry season, and a special trailer was designed which provided storage for the chairs and various items of equipment. These could be easily transported and quickly set up for the meeting. The trailer also proved its worth for children's work in various locations.

A New Convert

One of the first to be saved in Palapye was a man called RraSimole who heard the gospel in his sister's home. Jack Hay from Scotland was on his first visit and after preaching, he and others shared in the joy of witnessing RraSimole profess faith in Christ. The change in his life was evident to all. Sadly, his health deteriorated and claimed his life some months afterwards. The grace of God had rescued him before it was too late. Others who got saved were able to find fellowship in Serowe and be baptised there until Colin and Christine moved permanently to Palapye in 1999. They built a baptistry on their new site. Dan Gillies, another Scottish evangelist, gave much practical as well as spiritual help at that time.

Baptism

For about four years the Raggetts continued to attend the Serowe assembly and they enjoyed the fellowship and help of the believers from Serowe in their various forms of outreach in Palapye. The road between Palapye and Serowe can be dangerous, especially at night, with stray animals wandering about. Fatal accidents on major roads throughout the country occur frequently. One always appreciates the Lord's protection when undertaking any journey in Botswana.

A Suitable Site

In 1998, negotiations were begun to procure two adjoining sites which were for sale. Several buildings were included, one of which had immediate potential as a Gospel Hall. The other smaller site had already several residential buildings erected on it and these were suitable for a family home. The sites were conveniently located near a main road through Palapye. After the Raggett family moved there in October 1999, the first gospel meeting was held the next week in one of the small rooms that had been renovated and repainted for the purpose. Local people began attending.

The first Sunday School was held under a tree on the plot and a handful of children attended. Other buildings had been badly vandalised and were dilapidated. After many months of renovation work, including internal structural changes, several rooms became serviceable as additional classrooms and the main meeting room. Colin's experience in secular employment in the UK proved valuable in attending to these many practical tasks.

Sunday School

As numbers grew, so did the need for larger accommodation. Planning permission was obtained so that during 2001-2003, additional buildings were added including a new meeting room, a kitchen, and another classroom. The numbers attending the Sunday School grew year by year until about 800 children were attending. In 1999, a Bible Class began on Sunday afternoons and students from the Secondary School attended. Other gospel efforts among children have been conducted in the village in various suitable locations.

With the Lord beginning to bless the preaching of the gospel in Palapye, they began to first meet as a small assembly of seven believers in August 2003. Several visitors were also present on that happy occasion.

The Weekly Programme

At present, the weekly schedule involves the Lord's Supper on Sunday morning followed by a short prayer meeting before the preaching of the gospel. In the afternoon there is a Sunday School followed by the Bible Class. The gospel message is woven into the Bible teaching because many of the young people are not yet saved. In the late afternoon and evening, there is another time of prayer and Bible teaching. During the week, there is a Wednesday children's meeting followed by a gospel meeting. Every Saturday there is a Bible Reading conducted in the evening.

Using the national holiday period at the beginning of July, the Palapye assembly hosted several conferences with believers attending from all over Botswana. These were profitable and enjoyable, especially when fresh voices were heard as visiting speakers from overseas shared in the Bible teaching. As in other parts of Botswana, weddings of believers have been conducted in the Gospel Hall.

Work in Schools

It was as a result of a conversation that Beth Raggett had one Saturday morning in 1998 at the bookstall in Palapye town centre, that gospel work commenced in the Palapye primary schools. Beth was inviting some children to the meetings when their mother explained where they lived – it was too far away for the children to walk. The mother said, 'Why don't you go and see the headmaster of Sebeso Primary School? Speak to him about teaching the Word of God to the children in the school, because we don't want our children to go to hell.' An initial approach was made and the school proved welcoming. However, after speaking with the Regional Education Officer, permission was extended to teach the Scriptures in all of the state primary schools in Palapye. This opened a great door of opportunity.

For many years Colin had the privilege of teaching the four more senior classes in all of the eight schools every week. Children from all over Palapye began to hear the truth of the gospel and also became aware of the meetings in the hall. As is so common in Botswana, even after many years, young people introduce themselves as having once attended Sunday School and learnt many verses of Scripture. They never forget. This work eventually was brought to a close when the Education Officer explained that the teachers were complaining that time set aside for Bible lessons prevented them from completing the education syllabus.

Beginning in January 2000, opportunities were given to address school assemblies on three mornings of the week in three junior secondary schools. This amounted to speaking to several thousand young men and women each week. Colin Raggett was familiar to most of them from their earlier years spent in the primary schools. The scholars gave good attention to the message presented to them in Setswana.

School Assembly

English is used as the medium of instruction in the nearby Kgaswe International Primary School. Every Thursday morning during term time, the four senior classes hear the message of life. In common with other such schools in Botswana, these are private schools with higher fees. The children may be from wealthier families, but their spiritual needs are just the same as those who attend the state schools.

Sowing the Seed

Village schools outside Palapye have been visited from time to time. There have also been occasions when the '*Seed Sowers*' material has been widely distributed in the surrounding area. A team of volunteers from Palapye and elsewhere worked together in a concentrated effort over several days.

In recent months, the Serowe assembly has been visited each Thursday evening when the believers gather to pray and listen to Bible teaching. Shoshong is also visited on alternate Saturdays where Mavis's group of young people are keen to be taught the Word of God.

Training Programmes

Over the years, Christians from overseas have kindly helped young people in Palapye, sponsoring them to assist local businessmen in the town on a temporary basis. This has often led to them becoming permanently employed when they have proved their value to the business owners. Others have been able to train for a time in Colin Raggett's well-equipped workshop and they have assisted in property maintenance and improvements. The skills they acquire are valuable in the current job market.

An example of this was when the local secondary schools were suffering from a deficit of serviceable desks. In 2018, a programme was initiated to refurbish and repair school furniture in these and other schools in the town. This is an ongoing project which allows others to train and receive work experience. Sometimes repairs are made on-site, but usually, a large number of broken and discarded frames are transported to the workshop area beside the Gospel Hall where it is easier to complete the tasks. Hundreds of desks, stools, and tables have been reclaimed in this way and made serviceable again.

The Raggett children, Andrew, Phil and Beth, maintain their links with many of their friends in Botswana. Beth is presently teaching in a school in the UK and Andrew and Phil work together in their own company, organising self-drive tours of Botswana and neighbouring countries. As young boys, they were keen ornithologists and they were responsible for infecting many of us with their enthusiasm. Both are married with young families of their own. They visit Botswana as often as they are able and share in the work of the Lord.

Chapter 12

OTHER AREAS

While there are six established local assemblies of believers in Botswana, a great deal of work has been undertaken to reach out from all of these centres to other areas. Our hope has always been that souls will be saved, and new assemblies established elsewhere. The work in Serowe extended to a new area of the village, Goora-Leina, where a modern hall has been erected. In Gaborone, a second hall was erected on the western side of the city for outreach and there has also been blessing in Tlokweng village nearby and several outlying villages – Rasesa, Mochudi and Kopong. In Francistown, the local assembly work has extended to Tati Siding, Gerald Estates and Ntshe. In Selebi-Phikwe the village of Mmadinare has been evangelised as have the villages around Palapye and the town of Mahalapye to the south. In the Maun area, the people of Seronga and Shakawe have heard the words of life.

Reports from other African countries tell of thriving rural assemblies. To date, we have not seen the same kind of expansion in Botswana. It may yet come, even though there are several factors that make this seem difficult at present. We do believe that God can do what we consider to be impossible; He works in His own time and in His own way. Our responsibility is to keep sowing the seed.

Coping with Change

Traditionally, Botswana has been an agrarian economy. Even the national school holidays were arranged to allow children time to work in the fields and help their families with the harvest. This situation has changed. The younger generation seems to have much less interest in agriculture, at least the forms of subsistence agriculture where manual labour is a basic requirement. They may retain an interest in having cattle but even then, the cattle are looked after by an employee. Small farms have been amalgamated or bought up by those able to afford a more mechanised approach to commercial farming. The government is fully aware of this situation, but the trend is not so easily reversed as people continue to migrate to urban areas.

The education of young people begins in their home village at the local primary school. Their nearest secondary school is often found somewhere else, in a larger village. If they do well in secondary education, inevitably they move yet again and further away, either to the university in Gaborone or to the new tertiary institutions that are now being established in Francistown and Palapye. They may still retain strong links to their home village, but they spend most of their time away. If they graduate and enter the job market, their options are even more limited.

Concerning employment, jobs are now scarce. University students no longer graduate one day and the next day walk into a plush office to take up a well-paid post. In earlier years a good placement was virtually guaranteed. Today, competition for jobs often means an extended period of waiting. There are limited job opportunities for graduates in specialised subjects, particularly in a village setting.

One young man called Katlego Mazunga graduated in science and was offered a place to study for a higher degree. He declined this offer and returned to his home village of Serowe to set up a market garden project because he desired to help his local assembly. He has faced setbacks along the way but, so far, he has managed to support himself. For those who choose to train in manual skills such as building, carpentry, plumbing and electrics, enough work can be found locally. Their skills are exportable and in demand, even in a village setting. However, it is a minority of young people who choose this option. Desk jobs seem to be the goal of the majority.

Another factor is that those in government service have to be prepared for transfers. These can be disruptive to married and family life; inevitably, they affect assembly life as well. A husband can be sent to one area and his wife, if she is also employed by the government, may be posted in the opposite direction. There is no obligation for such transfers to be coordinated. Sometimes a wife has resigned from her post to keep the family intact.

Villages around Serowe

Jim and Irene Legge made good use of their clinic visits to outlying villages around Serowe. Initially, Paje, Mabeleapodi, Tshimoyapula, and Mashoro were on their itinerary. The distances involved and the nature of the bush roads in those days meant that only one place could be visited on any given day. There were opportunities to visit the schools in these villages and to conduct evening gospel meetings in the clinic buildings.

The presence of Ivan and Lenyora Mbangiwa in Mabeleapodi made it a favourite place for a stop. We recall the Sunday afternoon visits to their village with Jim and Irene to have a time of fellowship with them. Lenyora would make us tea. The local brand is called '*Five Roses*' but somehow her tea seemed so refreshing – even on a hot afternoon – that we renamed it 'Ten Roses'. Ivan was teaching in the local school, but later he was reassigned to another school in Nata, a northern village many miles away. Jim did have hopes of seeing the nucleus of a small assembly established there but this could not be realised. Another small village called Majwanaadipitse was the focus of interest for several years where the headmistress of the local school was keen for her pupils to receive instruction from the Bible. Again, with her transfer to a new area, the door closed. Mogorosi was yet another nearby village where the gospel was proclaimed.

Mochudi

This large village is about an hour away from Gaborone and it is the capital of the Bakgatla tribe. Their chief has sought to retain and promote tribal customs such as initiation ceremonies and circumcision. Gospel efforts have been conducted there over the years. When Heather Beggs moved there, the fenced property which she rented was an ideal site to pitch the gospel tent. Also valuable was her contact with local people through medical work in the district. We began to see blessing but almost exclusively among ladies or young girls.

One of our early gospel efforts involved hiring a school classroom in the centre of the village. We were assigned one of the older classrooms which was in a state of disrepair with broken windows and small battered chairs. It had no electrical supply, so our gas lamps were again put to good use. One of the older local ladies attended regularly – she used to sit at the front in her long winter coat and stare at us with a solemn look. That first year, there was no evident blessing, but we did feel that God had been speaking and convicting people of their need of salvation. The second year started off in the same way; however, before the end of the meetings, we had reason to rejoice when MmaCherika trusted Christ.

She became a different person. Now there was a smile, but more than that, she told us that we did not need to use the classroom any longer. We could use her home yard instead. This became a great blessing to us and over the years, regular gospel efforts have been conducted there in Morema ward. Her neighbour, MmaShirley, trusted Christ. Another lady next door was also saved. She died in a car accident after travelling to Gaborone to visit her daughter who was terminally ill in hospital. It was a sad duty to attend the joint funeral of the mother and her daughter a short time later.

Mochudi Ladies

One of the believers in the Gaborone assembly, MmaBoitumelo, owns a plot in Mochudi village and there we have held a large Sunday School for many years. MmaBoitumelo herself helped at the beginning. We also pitched the gospel tent there on several occasions. We used to rent her small house and have an overnight stay there each week. In more recent years we have been travelling out on Tuesday afternoon. Hazel holds the Sunday School on this plot while Joy has another children's class in Morema ward. Using MmaCherika's yard, I sit down with five older ladies, all believers who are now in assembly fellowship, and teach them the Scriptures. They do their best to travel into Gaborone at the weekends to join us in remembering the Lord, but they cannot be present at the other meetings, especially for teaching. Usually, five of their unsaved friends attend the Bible study so the gospel message is always included with the teaching. They all have shown a great aptitude for learning verses of Scripture, even though most of them have had only a basic education. Once again, menfolk are conspicuous by their absence.

A tragedy occurred some years ago. MmaBoitumelo's eldest son trained as a soldier. Being an intelligent young man, he was sent to the USA to study and qualify as a dentist. After returning to Botswana and completing his obligatory term of service in the army, he set up a private dental practice in Mochudi village. He married and had a little son. One morning his body was discovered hanging from the tree at the corner of her plot, under which we held the weekly Sunday School. No reason for his death was ever discovered – he left no note or any clue as to his state of mind.

The initial outcome was that the local children were too frightened to return to Sunday School. The neighbour was warning them that they would fall sick if they sat on the benches we had permanently installed under the tree for shade. Hazel decided to move the class to another corner of the plot but only a few children started to come again. One of the elders in the Gaborone assembly, Oitlogetse, felt that he should visit the neighbour and speak to her. He did so, telling her that our trust was in God and we need not fear. He read Scriptures with her and prayed. This seemed to have little effect. Children were still staying away. He returned and on the second occasion he spoke to the lady again, but this time he sat down on one of the benches under the tree. This had the desired effect of reassuring her. Little by little the Sunday School children returned until large numbers were coming as before. Our own words did little to change the neighbour's mind: 'You folks from overseas don't understand how we Batswana feel' was the response. There was some truth in this.

Shoshong

Reference has already been made to this important village: Khama III used it as his tribal capital and Fred Stanley Arnot stayed there for three months. It is located 25 miles west of Mahalapye and about 70 miles south of Serowe.

Our first visit to the village was made over 30 years ago when we were involved in the wedding of a fine Christian couple. The occasion was memorable for several reasons, not least for the moment when Jim Legge asked the customary question: 'Who giveth this woman in marriage?' The elderly man from the bride's side did not hear the question. Silence. The question was repeated with the same response. After a long pause, another old man in the middle of the congregation piped up: 'Well, if he won't, I will,' he said. After some moments of laughter and relief, the ceremony proceeded.

The ruins of the former village and mission station can still be visited. The valley is protected on three sides by a range of high hills. Visitors enjoy sounding the 'bell stone'. This large rock is found near the old kgotla and when it is struck with a smaller stone, it gives a clear ringing sound, just like a church bell. It was used to summon people to tribal gatherings.

Nurse Mavis Medupe comes from this village. She is now retired but she continues to contact young men and women with the gospel. A number of them have been saved. The village is now more accessible from Serowe and Jim Legge and other local brethren regularly travelled south on the new road to encourage Mavis and to teach the new believers. Her permanent presence there has helped to stabilise the work.

Mavis (back row in headscarf) and Young Believers

In recent years Mavis has opened her home to host a special week of evangelism. Brethren and sisters from other assemblies have come to support this and to help with the early morning (5.00 a.m.) Bible study, the afternoon tract distribution and open-air preaching, and the evening Bible study. It is a busy week. At such times, spiritual work can also be accomplished behind the scenes, through having personal conversations with young believers who are seeking counsel and direction in their lives.

Several schools in the village also receive the printed Bible lessons. Regular weekly visits continue to be made by the Serowe and Palapye brethren. Seabenyane Dichabeng and Colin Raggett alternate week about to give Bible teaching to the group of young believers. For a time, Mavis lived in Mahalapye, a major town on the main north-south highway. Different brethren have visited and preached the gospel there but so far there has not been evident blessing.

Lobatse

This town is located some 40 miles south of Gaborone. It was the first place in Botswana to boast a short section of tarred road. Over the years the gospel has been sounded out there using the homes of believers who have been sent there in government service and lived there for varying periods of time. Some have been teachers while others have been involved in the health service. Lobatse is where the Court of Appeals and the Department of Geological Surveys are based.

In more recent years, four families linked with the Gaborone assembly were living there. They were able to meet in a home during the week but would normally travel to Gaborone on Sunday to join the assembly of Christians for the day. Two families remain, the Bandas and Rabogadis, who remain active in the work of the Lord. They have a weekly Sunday School and are also able to visit local schools.

Ghanzi

This small town is situated in the middle of the Kalahari Desert, near the border with Namibia. A family from Gaborone, Nehemiah and Boitumelo Lekgetho and their five children were transferred on account of employment and for several years they made effective use of their home by organising a Sunday School for local children and meeting regularly with several other believers of like mind. Despite the large distances involved, a group of believers did make a trip to the town to help distribute gospel tracts.

The brother and his wife and family are now back in Gaborone (another government transfer) but we have seen that their personal experience of pioneer work has moulded them. They continue to have a real desire to share the gospel and see others blessed. Boitumelo is one of the ladies who helps each week to make up Sunday School prizes.

Ghanzi Bushmen Children

Sunday Schools

A notable feature of assembly life in recent years has been the interest of individual sisters to reach out to boys and girls in more isolated places. This has taken the form of a weekly Sunday School class. A lady teacher might be posted to a distant school in a small remote village. She may be there for only a few years, but she gathers the local children around her, perhaps under a tree, and faithfully teaches them the Scriptures. This is a lonely work in some respects, but we are sure that it will bear much fruit. Villages such as Mookane, Palla Road, Rasesa and Tsholamosese have all had such input.

With the frequent transfers in employment, there are challenges in continuing these various works. However, we rejoice that these sisters are making the best of their opportunities and we have no doubt that the sowing the seed of God's Word will not be in vain.

Tirelo Setshaba

New believers are taught early on in their Christian experience that they too are missionaries and with a responsibility to reach out to the unsaved with the gospel message. This conviction has produced blessing in unexpected places.

The national service scheme that used to operate countrywide, *Tirelo Setshaba* (Service to the Nation), meant that school leavers were sent to remote areas for a year to work amongst the people. This preceded their tertiary education in colleges or university. The scheme had many profitable outcomes although it also had certain risks for the participants, especially young women, being stationed alone in remote areas with little supervision or protection.

Several of our young men spent the year helping in village

schools or agricultural projects, but they boldly witnessed for Christ and souls were saved. In the southern village of Ramatlabama, a brother who was posted there saw a rich harvest of souls. A number of those who professed faith in Christ continued to make spiritual progress and today are valuable members of various assemblies.

To follow up the early work in Ramatlabama, I returned each winter for the next 10 years, lodging with a dear widow, the mother of Dan Keakantse who is now married and resides with his family in Scotland. Several young brothers shared in this work on occasions. Each day there was a Sunday School and later, an outdoor gospel meeting in a nearby yard, just before sunset. In all my time there I saw no obvious blessing. However, at the end of last year, I was asked to officiate at the wedding of a young Christian woman from the village. Her mother had also attended the adult meetings and she has since professed faith in Christ. The seed had been sown many years previously; the blessing came much later.

Ramatlabama Gospel Meeting

Two other young men, Letsibogo Molebatsi and Reuben Zilwa, were sent to two adjacent villages, Kopong and Lentsweletau. As a result of their testimony and witness, two schoolboys were saved. We were thrilled to discover that one of them was the grandson of Petros, the elderly gentleman who had been the night watchman on the site when we were building our first Gospel Hall in Gaborone. Contact was renewed with the old man, he heard the gospel again, and he was wonderfully saved, 20 years after first hearing the truth. This opened up the way for the work in Kopong to continue with opportunities to teach Sunday School and visit Petros for Bible teaching.

Principles of sowing seed are emphasised in Scripture: "He which soweth sparingly shall reap also sparingly; and he which soweth bountifully shall reap also bountifully" (2 Corinthians 9.6). A farmer who sows only half of his field cannot expect to reap more than half a field. But the one who sows the gospel seed widely and bountifully can rightly expect that God will give the increase and that one day there will be a great harvest.

Chapter 13

PREACHING

Preaching the gospel lies at the heart of missionary service. It is not an optional extra but rather the primary goal, as commanded by the Lord. There are many other valuable avenues of service that complement the declaration of the gospel, but these are secondary. Problems can arise when the priorities are altered.

The gospel is most effectively presented when the preacher's heart is full to overflowing with praise as he exalts Christ and His work upon the cross; God is honoured by this sweet incense ascending to heaven. Paul reminded the Corinthians that in gospel activity "we are unto God a sweet savour of Christ" (2 Corinthians 2.15). This is the language of worship.

The background picture was the welcoming parade for a Roman general returning from a triumphant military campaign in the distant regions of the empire. On that day, the general wore a laurel crown and a purple and gold toga. He rode in a chariot drawn by four horses. Ahead of him were the captive soldiers, shackled with chains, and then came the general himself. Following him were the victorious legionnaires shouting '*Io triumphe!*' (Hurrah for the Triumph!), the musicians playing their instruments and the priests waving their censers.

It was the incense from these censers wafting throughout the streets of Rome that Paul was alluding to as he wrote to the Corinthians. All the temples were to remain open that day; they too would have been permeated by the incense. To the exultant soldiers, it was the smell of life and victory; but to the captive prisoners, the same smell signified defeat and death. In the same way, the savour of uplifting Christ in the gospel not only brings pleasure to God and life to those who believe it, but it brings judgment upon those who reject it. Such are the weighty implications of proclaiming the gospel message.

In Botswana, we remain thankful for the liberty we have enjoyed for many years to proclaim the gospel. God has opened many doors in many places. Some of these doors have been opened for only a limited time so, as we look back, we are glad that we made use of them. We have had opportunities to preach not only in gospel halls but also in tents, in homes and yards, in the open-air on street corners in towns and under trees in villages. We have preached in schools, colleges and on the university campus, in clinics and hospitals, in prisons and refugee camps. We usually preach at weddings and at funerals. A few more unusual venues will be mentioned.

Preaching in Assembly Halls

Generally, adults do not flock to hear the gospel. Numbers can be small. Most of those who come have been personally contacted over an extended time. Women attend more readily than men. In Botswana, men prefer to stay in the company of other men in the evening, talking about politics, sport, or cattle, so it is unusual to see a man break from this tradition and attend meetings regularly. We preach the gospel at the weekends but also have a regular mid-week gospel meeting in addition to the open-air witness. Much work is required in contacting people, winning their confidence, inviting them and often transporting them to and from the meetings.

In the cities and towns of Botswana, there are no municipal road transport systems, even in the capital. Private minibus and taxi services can be unpredictable; they are not required to maintain strict time schedules. This is one reason for people sometimes arriving late. At night, there are security concerns about people walking home in the dark, and many believers have been robbed. If we are giving believers a lift home after an evening meeting, we try to drop them off at their front gate.

We recall with fondness the example Jim and Irene Legge set for us all as they frequently left their home an hour or so before the meeting time to navigate a long and circuitous route in pitch darkness, on rough, unmarked tracks throughout the village. Those of us who shared in this work had to quickly come to terms with such directions as, 'Turn left at the fallen tree, avoid the large pothole further up the track; turn right where you see the two boulders, and halfway up the hill you will see two thatched huts in a large yard with a kraal of goats under a syringa tree. Sound the horn twice and wait. The old granny does not hear too well.' After the meeting, the whole process was repeated. Jim was always glad of a chair and a mug of tea when he eventually arrived home.

Most of our converts have listened to the gospel for a considerable time before trusting Christ. It seems to take time for the fog of confusion and misunderstanding to be swept away before the light becomes clear. In our experience, the few who have made a quick profession and wanted to take the 'fast track' to spiritual growth have generally lost interest just as quickly. This does not change our belief that God can save a man or woman the first time they hear the gospel. We dare not limit Him.

Preaching in Goora-Leina

Our preaching is simple. It has to be. Today, over the airwaves and through social media, there is much religious propaganda being peddled. This has led to widespread confusion as to what the gospel is all about. The earnest preachers of a former generation did not miss the mark when they advocated that one should emphasise 'the three Rs' – man's ruin, God's remedy, and man's responsibility. Week in, week out, we share the preaching with local brethren. It is also our custom for two brothers to try to help an enquirer. In other words, we labour together in every aspect of the work.

One great truth of the gospel is that salvation is free of charge. It was paid for in full, long ago, by the precious blood of Christ. As

He hung upon the cross, the Saviour proclaimed, "It is finished" (John 19.30). This is one distinguishing feature that contrasts with the 'prosperity gospel' which has become so popular in Botswana as elsewhere. People flock to such meetings in pursuing a dream of personal health, wealth, and other temporal blessings. The emphasis is on the physical rather than the spiritual. Somewhere along the line, they are pressurised to part with their money in the hope of gaining more.

New government regulations have been introduced to try to limit and control religious charlatans who in recent years have flooded into Botswana and often fleeced the people. The legislation requires ministers of religion to have had training and certified qualifications that substantiate their credentials.

Preaching in Tents

In several locations in Botswana, tent work has been profitable. The brethren in Serowe, Palapye, Maun and Gaborone have at various times used this method of outreach and seen blessing. This can combine a children's meeting in the afternoon with a meeting for adults in the evening. Ideally, one should have a team of dedicated workers to help pitch the tent and others who are free to provide security, especially during the night when it is not being used. We have never had this degree of help unless we have hired a security firm to guard the property at night. In Botswana, tents constitute a portable business; people regularly rent them out for all sorts of occasions. Unless one's tent is guarded, it may be vandalised or even disappear. It is preferable to have it pitched in a fenced and gated area rather than on open ground.

Nevertheless, there have been profitable gospel efforts in various locations throughout Botswana. The Gaborone believers had several years of memorable tent meetings in the village of Rasesa, near Mochudi. These resulted in one after another of a particular family being saved. The village itself was a difficult place to work for several reasons. From time to time, after we had held the meeting and everyone was leaving the tent, under cover of darkness some local boys would assault the young folk we had transported to the meetings. There would be clouds of dust and audible scuffles, but nobody was seriously injured.

Travelling at night in the pitch darkness can also be dangerous with domestic animals roaming unattended. One night, when driving our minibus full of passengers, a donkey suddenly appeared from the left-hand side and began crossing the road. We struck it on the head and killed it – a few seconds later and we would have hit it full-on with perhaps more serious consequences. The Lord in His goodness preserved us.

Preaching in Homes

At times it is easier and more convenient to reach out with the gospel in locations where the people and their families live. Most of the assemblies in Botswana are familiar with this approach. There may be only one of the family saved but if other family members are agreeable, we gladly make use of these opportunities. The favourable weather in Botswana allows us to sit outdoors and have a meeting. The *lolwapa* (home yard) is often spacious and we can provide seats or benches so that the family and friends can come. In dark winter evenings, we use gas lamps or have a line of electric bulbs rigged up if electricity is available. A healthy measure of curiosity means that often a good number come at the beginning and listen at least a few times. Should their expectations of hearing lively music or seeing 'signs and miracles' not be fulfilled, they find excuses to absent themselves from the remaining meetings.

There are others, however, who are changed in a different way. One can almost tell by their faces. They keep coming but no longer seem so casual. As the preaching proceeds, they appear thoughtful, even concerned. What has happened is that the Holy Spirit has begun to convict them of their sin. When they begin to understand that they can do nothing to save themselves – it has all been done at the cross – there comes the moment when they trust Christ. The face that was showing anxiety and concern now beams with radiant joy and peace. It is a moment worth waiting for.

House Meeting

We regularly open up our homes to have 'cottage meetings'. These are aimed at giving our neighbours the opportunity to hear the gospel on home ground. Our friend and colleague,

Joy Griffiths, has often done this by using her flat in the large housing development where she stays. She works hard inviting not only her neighbours but also people she knows from various government offices or local stores. Our sister, Mavis Medupe, has also used her home with great effect wherever she has lived.

Preaching in the Open-air

In most towns and villages there is an open-air area sometimes referred to as 'freedom square' where people can speak publicly. It might be likened to Speaker's Corner in Hyde Park, London. It is always wise for us to seek permission beforehand. The Francistown assembly obtained permission to preach at numerous designated sites in one of the large housing developments in the city.

In Gaborone, we were permitted to speak once a week in the Broadhurst area in the north of the capital. For many years we held a Saturday morning meeting there in the commercial district, running an amplifier from a car battery. We stood behind a table with gospel literature and several large Setswana texts on display. Our brother and sisters would mingle among the passers-by and shoppers, offering gospel tracts. We know of several people who first heard the gospel in this way and then began attending the services in the Gospel Hall, eventually trusting Christ and becoming part of the assembly.

It is always necessary to be respectful. One Saturday morning, many years ago, a lady approached us as we were preaching. She began to ask probing questions about our church to which we replied politely. Towards the end of the conversation, we ventured to enquire as to her name. She told us, and then added, 'I am the Registrar of Societies for Botswana. Please come to my office on

Monday morning with your certificate of church registration.' We were relieved that we had not been either evasive or resentful in responding to her questions. On the following Monday morning, it was the same lady who reviewed our paperwork, confirmed our legitimacy, and treated us pleasantly.

There were other challenges along the way. A religious sect began standing just in front of us, as if they were part of us, and distributing their literature. People we met would first ask us if we belonged to their sect. From then on, we would make a short announcement at the beginning of our meeting, explaining in positive language who we were. (It is depressing to always have to define yourself negatively, by what you are not.) As the area expanded with more shops, these commercial premises began using large sound systems on the pavement to advertise their wares. It was not long before we were only a small part of a general cacophony that was drowning our voices. We decided to change our approach.

Open-air Gospel Meeting

For many years now the Gaborone assembly has conducted a weekly open-air meeting in the vicinity of the Broadhurst Hall. This continues throughout the winter and summer. We gather there and then walk to one of four sites in the low-cost housing areas near the hall. We are well known in the area because of our Sunday School. We set up a few benches, inviting local people to join us. Often, we have several neighbours sitting with us, but most adults listen from their homes, their porches and yards. Usually, we have a crowd of children at our feet. There are others walking home from work and they also hear. In wintertime, it is dark and cold, but it is heartwarming to be joined regularly by an elderly widow from the assembly who rarely misses a meeting. She sits wrapped up in her blanket, nobly supporting us as we preach.

Radio Work

We received an invitation to preach the gospel over the national radio system and for many years we used this opportunity. The national broadcasting would begin each day with a short prologue and end transmission at night with an epilogue. We would record seven Setswana messages at a time, for a week of either epilogues or prologues. There were also occasions when we recorded a full 25 minutes of preaching for the Sunday Service broadcast.

In the past, some of the speakers had abused this privilege and raised controversial and politically sensitive matters in their addresses. This resulted in a reduction of religious broadcasting time and a subsequent requirement that the messages be written out in advance, so that these could be previewed and censored if necessary. Our own contributions were never questioned or altered in any way.

With the introduction of national television and the commercialisation of public broadcasting, the format changed, and we were no longer invited or involved. And yet, we remain thankful for the years when the gospel was sounded out to every corner of the nation. In those times, before cell phones, it was customary for isolated communities and lonely people to have a radio always playing in the background. We hope that many listened and found the Saviour.

Special Occasions

While weddings and funerals are very different in regard to the occasion, the Word of God is appropriate to both. A young Christian couple publicly testify to their faith in Christ and their commitment to faithfulness in marriage. This gives us an opportunity not only to encourage the bride and groom but also to remind the onlookers why the particular couple have chosen this pathway.

At a funeral, it is always comforting to speak of the passing of a believer in the assurance that they are with Christ in a better place, heaven itself. It also provides an opportunity to remind the company that life is a journey and not a destination. Each one will pass the same way and so there is a need to prepare in good time to meet God. It has already been mentioned that in Botswana funerals are the best-attended social occasions with often hundreds of people present. Each evening, for up to a week preceding the day of the burial, dozens of local people gather for the *merapelo* (prayers). Usually, reverent attention is given to the Word of God.

Over the years, invitations to more unusual venues have given us an opportunity to read from the Bible and explain the truth of it. In our case, these places have included the local police station, the Sri Lankan embassy, a local wholesale business owned by Muslims, and a rehabilitation unit in the village of Tlokweng.

Throughout Botswana, the message is proclaimed, anywhere and everywhere, to anyone and everyone. There can be many months and years of sowing without evidence of blessing. It is God alone who can save; our part is to keep sowing. We take encouragement from cases that we know of in which the blessing came many years, even decades, after the first contact with the gospel. We believe heaven will be full of surprises.

Chapter 14

TEACHING

I will never forget my introduction to the disease known as kwashiorkor. In 1974, as a medical student on an elective attachment to Murchison Mission Hospital, South Africa, I was soon made aware of the devastating effects of this condition among the Zulu population. It is a severe form of malnutrition in children due to insufficient protein intake. In most cases, the children were receiving calories in their diet, but the all-important protein content was lacking. Their growth was stunted but, paradoxically, they appeared bloated. They were also weak, listless, and prone to infection. When treatment was delayed, many of them died. A well-balanced diet would have avoided these calamities.

The teaching of the Word of God is vital for the spiritual health and growth of all believers, but especially those who have recently come to faith in Christ. This teaching has to provide a balanced spiritual diet. Without the 'milk' and 'meat' of the Word, believers are weak and vulnerable to the attacks of the devil. The Lord Jesus Christ commissioned His disciples not only to evangelise but also to teach all of the things He had commanded. This dispels the notion that we should only be interested in conversions; there is a need for ongoing instruction in the Word of God. It implies a lifetime of labour to achieve a comprehensive result.

Furthermore, every believer has to be encouraged to apply and put into practice what they learn. The Lord Jesus Christ spoke of "teaching them to observe all things whatsoever I have commanded you" (Matthew 28.20). Knowledge itself is of no benefit if it is not translated into action; it may become a hindrance if it results in spiritual pride. The supreme goal of instruction in the Word is to become more like Christ.

Bible teaching needs to be regular and consistent if it is to be effective. It is the cumulative effect over time that makes the greatest difference. In Botswana, we encourage new believers to read the Bible every day and pray every day. This leads to a deepening of communion and one's relationship with the Lord. He speaks to us through His Word, and we speak to Him through prayer, in the manner of a two-way conversation. That is how we get to know Him better – by spending time with Him and having personal fellowship with Him.

Instruction in the Word of God also benefits from being systematic and consecutive. While flitting from one book to another, or from one favourite passage to another, is not unprofitable, the best outcome accrues from a structured and disciplined approach to Bible study. It was the apostle Paul who reminded the elders of the Ephesian church that when he was with them, he had not held back from declaring unto them "all the counsel of God" (Acts 20.20, 27).

Personal Bible Studies

New believers, like newborn babes, need the milk of the Word. This relates to basic Bible teaching, confirming them in their faith and giving them reassurance and guidance as to the way ahead. We have found it profitable to meet with a new convert in their own home to study the Scriptures together. This allows us to understand their home environment and the challenges they might face there. We can also meet other family members and begin to get to know them too. The study material can be tailored to suit the new believer's level of knowledge and their particular spiritual needs. They are free to ask questions if some matter is not clear. It is also useful to set them simple assignments so that they begin searching the Scriptures for themselves and become familiar with independent Bible study methods. One of the most valuable aspects of these times together around the Word is the development of a personal and enduring friendship.

Such studies are not meant to replace the normal teaching meetings in the assembly but rather to complement them. We cover foundational truths such as the assurance of salvation, prayer and Bible reading, baptism and the Lord's Supper, assembly fellowship and its responsibilities, the necessity of living a clean life and witnessing to others. In the context of Botswana today and the doctrinal confusion that abounds, we often give teaching about the Holy Spirit and spiritual gifts.

Even those brought up in a Christian family should not be assumed to understand these basic Bible truths. They have probably heard them many times over before they were saved, but without spiritual insight. It is wise to treat them in the same way as one would any other new convert, as a complete beginner.

Additional challenges can sometimes arise when trying to visit and encourage an elderly convert such as Petros from the village of Kopong. The main difficulty was that he was not able to read well, and he lived too far away to attend the assembly meetings regularly. He needed Bible teaching and I would visit him weekly.

After the customary greetings on arriving, I would enter his yard in the village and sit down beside him under his *mopipi* tree. Old gentleman that he was, he was usually dressed for the occasion in his waistcoat, with his hat and Bible on a little table, and his walking stick by his side.

Petros

We developed a particular way of working, with me reading short phrases of Scripture which he would repeat – he had a good memory – and then I would proceed with an explanation, again using short phrases which he would repeat. There could be several interruptions which I grew to enjoy: he might remember a story from his past when he worked in the mines in South Africa. We would take a break while he related the incident in all its detail. At other times, he would suddenly say, 'RraSethunya, let us sing together', and there would be another unscheduled break. His favourite Setswana hymn was a translation of 'Beulah Land', a hymn about heaven. After we had finished singing, we would then pick up the thread of our study again and proceed. Petros is now in heaven. I still miss him.

For over 25 years there was an opportunity to meet with students on the university campus for a weekly Bible study. Most of these young men and women were in assembly fellowship. Many Bible topics were covered in depth. The attendance varied according to the numbers of students who were enrolled in any given year. More recently, most of the students are expected to find accommodation off the campus so there is no longer the same number available or free to attend.

In the 80s, the student colleagues of a young brother in assembly fellowship, asked for a series of 'lectures on eschatology', as they put it. At nine o'clock in the evening, I found a mixed audience of about 70 students gathered in a lecture hall on campus. After a general introduction on the subject of prophecy and the various approaches to it, I explained that I would from then on be following what I considered to be the correct interpretation.

All went smoothly until I was dealing with the matter of the judgment seat of Christ following the rapture. When I said that a true believer could never lose salvation but he or she could lose their reward, there was a sudden uproar. Most of the student body who were in attendance immediately regarded me as a heretic and they vociferously let me know it! When the audience fell quiet for a moment, I offered them a choice. I would take up the subject there and then or proceed with what I intended to teach that evening and perhaps leave the last evening to consider the subject of salvation in detail. They opted for the second of these. The next week my audience had shrunk to less than 20 students and it never recovered after that. Just before the last evening, when we were to consider the issue of the eternal security of the believer, I received a message that the students had cancelled the meeting.

University Bible Study

Assembly Teaching

It is always a joy to see how God can raise up local brothers in the assembly who can open the Scriptures and expound them. The variety of gift means that there is also a variation in how different brothers approach a subject. On Saturday evenings in Gaborone, our custom is to meet for an hour and a half and after praying, one brother teaches from the Scriptures. For many years we travelled through the New Testament from Matthew to Revelation, and then repeated the process.

The Bible class format is different, allowing for audience interaction. Normally, after an introduction and initial teaching on a given subject, the brothers in the assembly can be invited to comment or ask questions. From time to time a younger brother may be given a short assignment for the following week. When he presents it in public, it is often clear that he has worked hard to search the Scriptures. In this way, we all learn, but he learns most of all.

We are accustomed to having alternating series of studies from the Old and New Testaments. Introductory studies on the structure of the Bible, the history of Israel and geography of the Holy Land were covered at various times. Typical teaching on the tabernacle, the High Priest's garments, the offerings, and the feasts were dealt with in a basic way as were the judges, kings, and prophets of Israel. Studies of the messianic Psalms and servant songs of Isaiah were included. The New Testament studies were mostly studies of individual books. From time to time other specific subjects such as assembly responsibilities, marriage and the home, tongues and healing, and prophetic matters have been dealt with.

The Bible Reading format can also be profitable when it is conducted in a way that benefits all of the members in an assembly. To expound individual Bible books or even passages of Scripture systematically means that even difficult passages are covered. Using one language is more convenient and freer flowing than trying to conduct a conversational study in two languages.

On a personal level, we soon discovered that a rethink was necessary concerning how we approached Bible instruction. It was a mistake to take anything for granted, and so we sought to build the foundation slowly, patiently, and carefully from the ground level up. This was not because the believers were slow to grasp the truth. Not at all! Many of them were more intelligent and quicker to learn than we had ever been. The issue was that they had not been taught basic Bible knowledge in childhood as had been our privilege. So, the preacher's phrase – 'you will know of course that …' was inappropriate and obsolete. Simplicity, conciseness and clarity were the keys to being understood.

Another necessary aspect of our teaching was being prepared to enquire from time to time whether or not we had been understood. Sometimes, even after labouring to present a truth clearly, we discovered to our dismay that we had completely missed the mark. The fault was not that of our listeners, it was ours – 'Back to the drawing board!'

Bible Conferences

These special times of joyful fellowship are valuable. We tend to use the national holiday periods for these conferences as they allow people to travel the large distances involved and spend several days together. The holiday weekends are particularly busy on the roads and so it is no vain prayer that seeks God's protection on the journey. Police checks are more prominent at these times and by painful experience, we have learnt to make sure that our vehicle registrations are up to date and the vehicles themselves are roadworthy, otherwise, they can be impounded.

A convenient pattern developed with Serowe usually hosting the Easter conference. A shorter holiday at the beginning of July (Seretse Khama Day) has allowed the Palapye assembly to be hosts on several occasions. The mid-July conference weekend (President's Day) has been hosted annually by the Gaborone assembly, and the Francistown assembly has often hosted a conference at the end of September (Independence Day).

Attendances can vary but often around 300 people are present; occasionally, the number is significantly larger. The visiting brothers and sisters and their children have to be accommodated and fed over the three days. The believers of the hosting assembly prepare their homes to receive their older friends from distant assemblies; most of the young people are accommodated at the hall, sleeping in various classrooms or even using the main hall if no other space is available. These are precious times of fellowship, allowing friendships to be formed or renewed. This is important for the young as well as the old. The large distances between the assemblies mean that for most of the year we do not see one another.

Visiting Bible teachers have been a great blessing to the Christians in Botswana. A fresh voice is always welcome. Several overseas speakers have made repeated trips and they feel more 'at home' in our country. They have become accustomed to speaking by interpretation, they know the names and faces of many believers and have often chatted to them. They have even grown to enjoy our food athough it is quite different from overseas conference cuisine.

Large cooking pots over wood fires are much in evidence at conference time. The ladies are experts at controlling the intensity of the flame by rearranging the pieces of burning wood underneath. A typical menu will have a thick porridge made from ground corn (*paleche*) or rice, accompanied by beef or chicken, with green vegetables and gravy. The men are involved too, not only chopping the wood but also helping to lift the heavy pots and showing off their skills at pounding the cooked beef in the pot until it shreds. The end product is the special menu item that all Batswana love – *seswaa*!

Conference Speakers and Interpreters

As far as spiritual food is concerned, many believers look back to conference times when God spoke to them in a special way. It is also encouraging for those serving the Lord in Botswana to have visiting overseas speakers reaffirm truths that have been taught locally for many months and years. Local believers may sometimes wonder if Christians in other countries believe and practise the same things that they do? They are reassured that this is indeed the case. As to further blessing, not a few people have attended conferences initially as unbelievers and God in His grace has saved them. The gospel is always sounded out alongside the Bible teaching.

Helpful Literature

Over the years, various Bible study materials have been written in Setswana and others translated into the language. These have been widely distributed to the believers and have included a Bible dictionary, introductions to both Testaments and individual books of the Bible, teaching on discipleship, marriage and the home, and other issues relevant to the society in which we live.

One of the early believers was an elderly man most of us did not know. His name was Rre Maruping and he lived in the village of Tonota, quite a distance from other believers. Jim and Irene Legge came into contact with him and he trusted Christ. They were able to make occasional visits to encourage him.

As far as teaching was concerned, he had limited opportunities except that an excellent book had just been translated into Setswana, *The Church of the Book* (Everyday Publications). Dr Ed Harlow had crafted an engaging story about a group of new believers who were left very much to their own devices. All they had was the Bible and a shared desire to obey it. Slowly but surely, and step by step, they learned how the first Christians lived and practised their faith. Guided by the Holy Spirit through the Scriptures, they faced each issue as it came up. They searched their Bibles for the answer and made steady progress. Rre Maruping was enthralled by this account and was greatly blessed by having this resource. Along with his Bible, this instruction fortified and kept him going. He would often refer to it. We were privileged to be invited to preach at his large funeral in 1983.

Conference Book Table

Other Media

One Irish preacher from a former generation was honest enough to admit in public that he had once considered recorded ministry in a negative light; however, he confessed that he had since changed his mind. In the days when it was safe to give a lift to strangers or hitchhikers, he used to play tapes of gospel messages when there was a grateful passenger alongside. Another humourist quipped that we, who had once been known as bookworms, were fast becoming tapeworms!

The world has moved on since then, from tapes to CDs, and now MP3 files. All kinds of recordings as well as reading material, good and bad, can be accessed via the internet – we have to be fearfully aware of the spread of evil of every kind through this medium. At the same time, nothing about human nature has changed, and the spiritual need is greater than ever. We seek to do what we can to spread the gospel and the truth of the Word of God through these various media.

In Botswana, we began recording conference ministry and other helpful messages. Tapes were prepared and sent to believers who had missed out or who lived in isolated places. Joy Griffiths had a special machine that copied several tapes at once. Sometimes it was in danger of going up in smoke because of overuse. Others took up the work. Franklin McIlroy and John Bandy were instrumental in preparing and distributing CDs of ministry on a wide variety of topics from different speakers, including those who are now in heaven. It is always a joy to listen to these men of a former generation who laboured to help us understand the Scriptures of truth.

Since the beginning of the global pandemic in 2020, we have made wide use of technology to spread the gospel and the teaching of the Scriptures. This has helped believers keep in touch, especial those who are lonely and are prohibited from meeting physically with others. With lockdowns and curfews, normal assembly meetings have been limited. In Botswana, we are aware that many believers still do not have an internet connection. We are burdened to keep in touch with such by phone calls or when permitted, occasional personal visits. We maintain social distancing while we pray with them and pass on a word of encouragement from the Scriptures.

The Word of God is described as being incorruptible seed "which liveth and abideth for ever" (1 Peter 1.23). Whereas "heaven and earth shall pass away", God has declared that "my words shall not pass away" (Matthew 24.35). The Bible teacher is dealing with issues that are eternal. There is nothing so important.

Chapter 15

SHEPHERDING

In our home village of Tlokweng, we are accustomed to seeing domestic livestock wandering freely and unattended from place to place, necessitating great vigilance when driving, especially at night. You might turn round a corner and suddenly come upon a herd of cows lying in the middle of the road, seemingly unconcerned. They are best regarded as a roundabout and negotiated accordingly. The goats have usually returned safely to their kraal by the evening. However, it is the sheep that require the most care: they are prone to wander and get into trouble. Without a shepherd, they are in danger.

Preaching the gospel results in salvation. Teaching the Word of God provides spiritual nutrition. But beyond this, the ministry of shepherding gives direction and protection: guiding and guarding God's people are vital for their spiritual welfare. Shepherding is not a ministry confined to a few hours a week spent in a church building, but rather it covers all the various physical and spiritual needs of believers at all other times. It is a wide-ranging ministry, demanding time and energy.

Christ the Example

The Bible uses the metaphor of sheep and shepherding to remind us that we were once lost and intent on going our own way: "All we like sheep have gone astray; we have turned every one to his own way" (Isaiah 53.6). God in His love sent His Son to seek us and to save us (Luke 15.4; 19.10). The Lord Jesus Christ described Himself as the *Good Shepherd* who gave His life for the sheep (John 10.11). This refers to His sufferings on our account when He died upon the cross of Calvary. We who have trusted in Him come to understand that not only has He suffered for us, and sought and saved us, but He secures us by His power: "I give unto them eternal life; and they shall never perish, neither shall any man pluck them out of my hand" (John 10.28). We are eternally safe and secure in His mighty hand.

If Christ's title as the Good Shepherd reminds us of His death, His designation as the *Great Shepherd* reminds us of His resurrection. We might well ask, 'What good would a dead shepherd be?' With such a perplexing question in mind, the Lord Jesus reassured His disciples that, even though He would lay down His life for them, He would take it up again: "I lay down my life, that I might take it again. No man taketh it from me, but I lay it down of myself. I have power to lay it down, and I have power to take it again" (John 10.17-18). Having saved us, He now lives to sustain us. This is His present work. The author of Hebrews reminded his readers that it was "the God of peace, that brought again from the dead our Lord Jesus, that great shepherd of the sheep, through the blood of the everlasting covenant" (Hebrews 13.20).

Christ is also described as the *Chief Shepherd*, and this points forward to His return in glory: "And when the chief Shepherd shall appear, ye shall receive a crown of glory that fadeth not away" (1 Peter 5.4). Until that day dawns, Christ has delegated authority to godly men whom the Holy Spirit has raised up to continue to care for the flock. (They are also known as "elders", signifying spiritual maturity, and "overseers", signifying watchfulness, Acts 20.17, 28.) They could be considered as under-shepherds, subject to the sovereign control of the Chief Shepherd, their Lord. One day He will return in manifest glory and reward them for their faithful stewardship.

'The Loving Shepherd'
Gospel Tract

The Need in Botswana

At the beginning of a pioneering gospel work, one individual may seem to be doing almost everything.[4] This is not by choice but of necessity, especially if he has to work alone. He must diligently seek out the lost wherever they are. He then faithfully and lovingly presents to them their need as sinners and Christ's ability to meet that need. His great burden is that God will be pleased to bless by saving souls who will one day be able to share in the work. When the first souls are saved, there is great rejoicing! Now another responsibility arises: new believers have to be taught the Word of God and guided on the Christian pathway. This is an ongoing work requiring years of patient instruction by life and by lip. It can only be sustained by love.

The ultimate goal is that a local assembly of Christians will be established by God's grace and that the Spirit of God will raise up faithful men as shepherds to diligently care for the sheep. The recognition of such men cannot be rushed. Gift takes time to develop, but the demonstration of public gift in preaching and teaching the Word of God is never enough in itself; it is to be exercised with humility and applied with consistency.

Shepherds are those who care for the flock and constantly sacrifice their time and energy for the blessing of others. They will have been demonstrating this caring attitude long before they are formally recognised. Furthermore, they do this 'off the platform' as well as when they stand up publicly to teach God's Word. Indeed, most shepherding takes place 'behind the scenes'.

Shepherds are servants, not lords. Mistakes will be made if, out of expediency, young men are thrust into prominence just because of their education, eloquence, or intelligence. Pride and self-importance are constant dangers (1 Timothy 3.6). What these men will require more than anything else are a lowly spirit and a tender shepherd heart. As they feed and tend the flock – bringing back the wandering, lifting up the fallen, binding up the broken, and much else besides – they will remember that they too were once lost and wandering sheep. They are not confidently self-reliant; they are God-reliant men of prayer.

Faithful shepherds lead the sheep to good pastures and fresh water, just like the Shepherd of Psalm 23. In the context of a local assembly of Christians, the elders make sure that there is a balanced spiritual diet of Bible teaching that will strengthen and refresh the believers. In Botswana, new converts are vulnerable to erroneous teaching that can unsettle them and cause them to doubt: 'Can I lose my salvation? Do I need to speak in tongues? Can a Christian be demon-possessed? Why am I not healed? Am I missing out on becoming rich and successful? Must I keep the Sabbath day?' These kinds of questions can perplex those that are young in the faith.

Families

Apart from the basic need for elders to organise and provide regular and systematic teaching for the assembly, they have other important responsibilities. Some of these are unusually challenging and put the elders' spirituality and wisdom to the test. There are times when elders can feel totally inadequate, lacking in full knowledge of a particularly difficult situation and aware of their own inability to address it. Their only recourse is to lay hold upon God in prayer.

It is comforting to recall God's word to Moses and his helpers: "Ye shall not respect persons in judgment; but ye shall hear the small as well as the great; ye shall not be afraid of the face of man; for the judgment is God's: and the cause that is too hard for you, bring it unto me, and I will hear it" (Deuteronomy 1.17).

Guiding

Elders make decisions together on behalf of the assembly. When they do so, they keep in mind the whole company of believers and not just the needs of a particular group. An assembly is not a democracy; it functions as a group of different individuals united by their submission to the Lordship of Christ and the authority of His Word. Elders seek to understand the mind and will of God for the way ahead; they do not need to canvass support or lobby for their point of view. When they are sure of God's will, they can confidently move forward.

Teenagers

Through the teaching of the Scriptures, believers learn how to live to please God. He calls us all to a life of devotedness and holiness. At times there are other more personal issues that people may bring to the attention of one or more elders. Young people often seek counsel regarding life choices and a possible career. Elders will encourage them to seek a job in which they can honour God and also give regular help in the local assembly.

There is also the matter of personal relationships and finding the right partner for marriage. It is important to give counsel to a young person or a couple before their wedding day. This will involve reading the relevant Scriptures and also passing on advice which perhaps has been learned the hard way, in the school of experience.

At other times, counselling might include a warning of potential dangers on the Christian pathway. The apostle Paul reminded the Ephesian elders how that for three years he had not ceased "to warn every one night and day with tears" (Acts 20.31). He pointed out the dangers from outside and those from inside the assembly. His concern was for the unity of the local church; he knew it could be easily disturbed. His shepherd care for the Ephesians was expressed in public instruction and in private counselling, from house to house (Acts 20.20).

Sensitive personal matters have to be dealt with confidentially. Believers must be sure that their concerns and problems are not broadcast to others. This is fundamental. Elders are meant to be not only approachable and sympathetic, but also men of integrity.

Encouraging

It is easy to become discouraged on the Christian pathway,

especially when personal or assembly problems arise. Elders are there to strengthen those who might feel dejected and need to be 'carried' for a time.

Elders also encourage the development of gift among young men and women. The public gifts of preaching and teaching take time to develop and they require opportunities to use them. This cannot happen if the elders are the only ones to speak in public. All of us owe a debt of gratitude to those with shepherd hearts who spurred us on when we were young in faith. Even though we made mistakes along the way, they were patient with us and continued to love and care for us. They saw the potential for better things and faithfully supported us. Our Lord's treatment of his stumbling disciple, Peter, is a reminder of His tender heart.

Other gifts may not be public, but they are just as important. The sisters in an assembly have a vital role to play and it is well recognised that often they form the spiritual backbone of a local church. This is true in Botswana as in many other countries. Their faithful attendance at the meetings and their interest in all aspects of assembly life encourage everyone. Their kindness and thoughtfulness, often expressed behind the scenes in personal visits, can make all the difference to those who are downhearted. Their prayers have great influence and bring down the blessing of God upon the preaching of the gospel. Both men and women need to be appreciated for their unique contributions to assembly life.

Supporting

There are times when emotional and practical support is necessary for those who face an acute crisis in their lives. It may be a bereavement, illness, or unemployment. The practice of the early church as well as the teaching of the apostles emphasised the responsibility of offering material support to those who were in need. The elders take the lead at such a time, visiting the bereaved to comfort and encourage them, and passing on financial support on behalf of the assembly.

After a family bereavement here in Botswana, the assembly rallies round and helps with purchasing food supplies for the evening snacks after the nightly 'prayers' and the main meal on the day of the funeral. The sisters also assist with cooking and serving. The brethren may be called upon to share in other practical tasks. There is a lot of work to do.

Assembly Widows

There is a large number of widows in the assemblies here as well as older women who are unmarried but have borne children before conversion. These ladies can struggle to cope and it is a privilege to be able to help them in a time of need. This is done quietly and discreetly. The Lord has always had a love and concern for widows, orphans and strangers. It was shown by His provision for these vulnerable groups in the nation of Israel

(Leviticus 19.9-10; Deuteronomy 24.19-20); it was also evident in the early church (Acts 6.1-3). Love for the Lord is reflected in love for His people.

Steadying

We use this word concerning times when storms come, speaking figuratively. Prevailing winds of opposition and strife can rock the assembly, disturbing the peace and threatening to shake the faith of some. Steady hands are required to guide the saints through the crisis. When the apostle Paul was caught in a real storm on the Mediterranean Sea, Luke records how the mariners sought to use "helps", ropes or cables that were passed beneath the hull and secured on either side to undergird it (Acts 27.17) This too is a picture of the work of elders. They keep the assembly on a true course and work hard to hold it together.

In the history of the children of Israel, when ten of the twelve spies gave an alarming report about the enemy giants they had seen in the land of Canaan, it was a man called Caleb who "stilled" the people and encouraged them not to look at the obstacles but to look up to the Lord (Numbers 13.30). Every assembly of Christians today needs people like Caleb who can encourage them to continue moving forward and to keep trusting in God.

When there are troubles from within, the devil attempts to cause division. The rebellion of Korah was a challenge to the nation of Israel, when he and his associates sought to usurp the established rule of God as represented by Moses and Aaron (Numbers 16.2-3). The disaffected group complained about the leadership and implied that these two men were only interested in holding on to power. Moses fell on his face and appealed to

God. It was God who intervened to uphold the honour of His name, with judgment falling swiftly and decisively on the rebels.

It will be no surprise that the short history of the work of the Lord in Botswana as recorded in these pages has not all been 'plain sailing'. There have been times of great stress and strain when the devil has sought to destroy what God has established. There have been sleepless nights, anguish of mind and heart and many tears. Through it all, God has been faithful.

Restoring

Shepherds carry a heavy burden of care. They are cheered when they see believers, young or old, making spiritual progress. They are troubled when they observe others who are lagging behind and beginning to wander; nevertheless, they are not always successful in recovering those who stray. Despite their sincere and best efforts, some are determined to take their own way.

At times believers can fall into sin that requires assembly discipline. There may be moral failure or doctrinal error involved. This is the painful and distressing side of leadership in a local assembly. Preceding such a decision made on behalf of the assembly, a careful enquiry has been made to make sure that the correct facts are known. There should be no haste in this regard. However, there should be no delay when it is time to act. To overlook sin means that the testimony of an assembly is compromised and defiled. The story of the man called Achan in the days of Joshua reveals that hidden sin can weaken the whole company and endanger the safety and progress of others (Joshua 7.11-12).

A great deal hinges on an individual's response to assembly discipline. Some may refuse to see the elders when requested to do so; eventually news comes back that they have joined another group. This evasive response is never the answer that leads to spiritual recovery. Others may agree to meet with the elders but become resentful of the discipline, casting blame on others. They may try to engender support for their viewpoint and paint the elders as being harsh and the assembly as being unloving. This antagonistic response reveals more about the individual than about those trying to deal with a difficult situation.

We look back with thankfulness to the times we have witnessed true repentance in those who have been disciplined and put out of the fellowship. They have humbled themselves, confessing their wrong and showing their preparedness to accept the discipline. Gradually, over weeks and months, they have continued to quietly attend the assembly meetings and thus regained the confidence of the believers. They have not engaged in gossip or created factions, but by their acceptance and submission, they have shown that they are earnest about being restored to the Lord and to the assembly.

The day comes – a joyous day it is – when the believer is received back into the assembly. This has happened on a number of occasions and it is a matter of great thanksgiving. Even better is to see the restored brother or sister making up for lost ground and once again showing evidence of growing in grace and in the knowledge of our Lord Jesus Christ.

The Joy of Shared Responsibilities

We are grateful for those men with shepherd hearts whom God has raised up among the assemblies of Christians in Botswana. The wisdom of having a plurality of elders in each assembly has been seen again and again. Following the New Testament pattern, their different gifts are blended together for the benefit of all. Mutual encouragement and accountability serve to strengthen and bind us together. It is a joy when a group of men work harmoniously together, not only learning from one another but also sharing the highs and lows of serving the Lord and caring for His flock.

Chapter 16

LITERATURE WORK

In most developing countries there is a thirst for reading material. In the early years of the work in Botswana, there was very little material available in Setswana. Jim and Irene Legge were burdened to begin addressing that need. Initially, they were assisted by Dr Merriweather who arranged for the translation of several of their first Setswana gospel tracts.

Gospel Tracts

A gospel tract has a life of its own. If a person is offered one and accepts it, it is like a dormant seed awaiting the right time and the right conditions when it can suddenly burst into life. As others have pointed out, it perhaps enters a home and remains there until the recipient is alone and in a reflective frame of mind – 'Well, what does this little paper say?' A well-written tract is relevant, pointed, and contains the living Word of God. It does not argue, compromise the truth, or grow discouraged as a person might. It can be read and reread. Even if the recipient discards it or leaves it unread, someone else can pick it up, read it, and receive a blessing.

In Botswana, the good services of the Evangelical Mission Press in Cape Town were used initially in producing the growing number of Setswana tracts. The whole process took more time in those days and depended upon the efficiency of the postal service. Technical progress moved forward in stages: manual typewriters were replaced with electric ones, but still the ubiquitous correction fluid was close to hand. Jim purchased a spirit duplicator to assist in preparing Bible notes for the assembly believers in Serowe. He and Irene then acquired their first word processor, and it seemed a wonder to us all to watch Irene printing a short phrase that scrolled in front of her on a minute screen. Soon afterwards, two new Amstrad computers (PCW8512) made their way across the ocean to Botswana, and Jim and I felt as if we had landed on the moon. The dedicated word processor now displayed a complete page of green script that could be saved and later edited – no more Tippex!

Gospel Tracts

Dozens of new tracts were added to the list. The presentation and content were tailored to meet local needs. There would be special events that could be commemorated with a relevant link to Scripture. There were tracts written especially for the sick and sorrowing, and for children and young people. Others touched on particular social problems or challenges that the people of Botswana were familiar with. When the Legges eventually acquired the ability and technology to do their own printing, it was a great boon for us to be able to write a new Setswana tract, typeset it, send it by email to Serowe, and within a few weeks the tract was available for distribution. In more recent years, when books, larger print jobs or full-colour printing have been required, we all have found it convenient to use local commercial printing companies.

As mentioned previously, in December 2018 Jim and Irene had driven the 200 miles to Gaborone to collect a large consignment of gospel literature they had ordered from a local printer. On their return, they had a fatal accident and Irene was called home to heaven. The truck had overturned, leaving the roadside covered in gospel leaflets that told of the love of God. Even in death, Irene had spread the words of life.

For many years we received a supply of laminated pocket calendars from Northern Ireland. These were printed in English but we were also provided with our own special Setswana version. Ed Jaminson generously printed and posted them out to us. We now produce our own. These are always gratefully accepted; no one has ever been seen throwing one down on the ground. They are also eagerly awaited every year. We are often asked months in advance: 'When will we have our new calendars?' They reappear in all sorts of places – stuck on the walls of government offices, posted on the glass dividers at the post office counter, or pasted on the book covers of the schoolchildren. Parents love them too because we manage to incorporate the names of the months in both Setswana and English, and we indicate the national holidays. On the other side is a pointed gospel message. It has become our custom to always include the same short phrase at the bottom of the calendar – 'Modimo O a go rata' (God loves you).

In Palapye, Colin Raggett was able to prepare a Setswana version of the 'Seed Sowers' material. This venture has previously gone forward in many other countries, particularly North and South America, and its basic aim is to provide homes with an attractively presented gospel text of John 3.16 in the local language. Colin put his artistic skills to good use in preparing the full-colour image. A small explanatory leaflet explains the meaning of the verse. Large quantities of these texts have been distributed, particularly in Palapye and the surrounding areas.

For over three years, Franklin and Jenny McIlroy were based in Serowe where Franklin was quick to learn the two-colour Riso printing technique. He was able to share the burden of the printing work with Irene. In 2009, they printed 450,000 lessons and tracts. Franklin also arranged for the commercial printing of a wide selection of gospel texts in full colour, as well as various Setswana gospel booklets. We continue to distribute these useful materials widely.

Even those who made short visits to Botswana have shared in the literature work. Friends from South Africa provided a reprint of a gospel booklet for children. Another visitor, Eunice Strahan from Northern Ireland, returned to her home country with a selection of superb images she had captured with her camera. These photographs returned to Botswana as attractive laminated gospel texts; these have been received by thousands of children and their parents. Only eternity will reveal the full harvest of those whose lives have been changed forever through reading a gospel tract, calendar, or picture text.

Correspondence Courses

The Legges had several Emmaus courses translated at the beginning of their work. These were at a basic level with a gospel emphasis and were distributed personally to local contacts. Jim found them useful in gauging a person's understanding of gospel truth. Their vision expanded as they sought to reach out widely to other areas of Botswana by setting up a new and culturally appropriate work – 'Sunday School by Correspondence' (*Sekole sa Tshipi ka Tlhaeletsanyo*).

The gospel lessons began at a very simple level but they gradually became more advanced. On a short visit to Canada in 1992, the Legges were able to meet Ed and Gertrude Harlow. Even in their 'retirement', this elderly couple worked hard each day on their small laptops, writing new Bible teaching material for Everyday Publications. This was a 'faith' venture set up by Dr Harlow to provide suitable literature for the mission field and areas where English for most people is a second language. Jim and Irene returned to Botswana with a desire to do more.

A new building was erected on the Serowe Gospel Hall site and this housed a print room and storeroom. Two computerised printing machines as well as a guillotine and folding machine were purchased. Irene became an expert at the whole process and spent many long hours, head down in her inimitable way, labouring diligently to fill the shelves with the necessary materials. She was able to do two-colour printing. An older local sister from the assembly, MmaLetsibogo, also assisted and gave years of faithful service, helping to fold, pack and store the tracts. Other believers gave occasional help along the way as they were free and able. The office staff expanded as the work grew. Tshepiso Sesinyi and Lebogang Puso formed the original team; several others joined later. Tony Haughton from England paid several visits to Botswana to assist Jim with computerisation of the records and related matters. His help and fellowship were greatly appreciated by all.

The Print Room in Serowe

The Sunday School lessons began to find their way to all parts of Botswana and the workload was considerable in terms of registration, receiving, marking, commenting, and returning the material along with the next lesson. Thousands of courses are now sent out each month. In those initial years, the postal service was speedier than it is today. The lessons became popular in schools and the interest extended to include some teachers who were just as keen as their pupils. In more recent years the distribution method has changed; the lessons are mostly delivered personally to primary and secondary schools in Serowe and the surrounding district. Two brothers, Seabenyane Dichabeng and Michael Ketshwereng, make regular road trips to these schools, the furthest being 75 miles away. The sisters usually remain in the office and continue with the necessary administration. All of these believers have felt burdened to keep this valuable work going, even after Jim and Irene's passing. This team of volunteers has heard of several enrolled students professing faith in Christ recently.

The gospel lessons have now been augmented by a full set of in-depth lessons, one hundred in all, called *The Way of Righteousness*, compiled by the late Ken Jones of Brazil. These are aimed at assisting and building up new believers; they are replete with sound teaching and are made available in both Setswana and English. Richard Wallace from Peterhead in Scotland was able to make a personal visit some years ago and since then he has continued to give invaluable help in making these materials available online in English (*https://biblelessons.online*). The introductory webpage encourages new students to 'Join our 20,000 Happy Students Today!'

In 1987 Jim began printing a local Setswana magazine called *Maungo* (fruit). This provided Bible teaching relevant to life in Botswana. A lot of work was required to prepare and issue it quarterly. Local brethren from other assemblies were invited to contribute and a wide variety of subjects were covered. Short reports of the Lord's work in Botswana were included from time to time. The magazine was produced regularly for over 30 years.

Book and Booklets

Many books and booklets have been written and translated into Setswana. These are too numerous to list individually, but as well as gospel subjects these also have covered many aspects of Christian life and service. Translation work is slow and painstaking. One must achieve accuracy and clarity but also a free flow of language that will be easily read and understood by a local person. The translation must always be checked by a national believer.

Topo Moleele was a young lady boarding at Swaneng Hill School in Serowe. Jim regularly visited the school to speak to the students, and on a Saturday afternoon it became his custom to have Topo's assistance in checking the Setswana messages he would later preach. School leavers at that time were required to do a year of national service and Jim suggested that Topo might wish to work as a translation assistant during her gap year. The application was approved and she joined the office team in April 1991. What was meant to be only a year in the office extended to over ten years, until June 2002.

Topo proved to be gifted in translation work and a stream of excellent materials and resources were produced. All of us throughout Botswana benefitted immensely. Emmaus courses written by William MacDonald as well as material written by Dr Ed Harlow in Canada for Everyday Publications were found to be appropriate to our needs. Everyday Publications used every day English!

We love to sing in Botswana and we do so with natural harmony. We found that compiling our own hymnbooks set a tone for our assembly meetings. The first hymnbooks were a simple affair: the pages were simply photocopied and bound with two staples. These were inexpensive to make but not so durable for frequent use. After moving to Francistown, Ian Rees produced a hardbacked hymnbook with both Setswana and English hymns. In the following years, Jim and Irene with Topo's help gave us three hymnbooks in Setswana: *Hymns of Worship, Hymns for Believers,* and *Gospel Hymns.* Writing or translating hymns is exacting work requiring a special range of skills. It was not uncommon for Jim to have attended a local funeral where he heard a beautiful traditional hymn tune. He would later repeat the tune to Topo who would get down to work and craft her own words, words that touch the heart. Many of us, when we sing these local hymns in remembrance of our blessed Lord, sometimes struggle to hold back a tear.

Several years ago we completed and printed a Setswana translation of Bert Cargill's helpful book published by John Ritchie Ltd. of Kilmarnock, *Tell me more about the Gospel.* In Botswana, we have a statutory requirement that the National Library and University should receive several copies of all the books we produce. After fulfilling this requirement with Bert's book, a request came from the National Library for a further 50 copies. This had never happened before. We hope and pray that these were widely distributed and read with profit throughout the country.

Bibles

While being committed to using Setswana, we are aware that Botswana is changing, and the school children are becoming more fluent in English from an earlier age. Large gifts of Trinitarian Bibles and children's Bibles from overseas have been widely distributed, particularly to those with whom we have personal contact. Joy Griffiths was able to visit the schools in Gaborone where she teaches, and present each school-leaver with a personal copy. Others have done the same in their own localities.

There have been also occasional opportunities to pass on Bibles personally to several of our state presidents: the late Sir Ketumile Masire in Gaborone and more recently, President Ian Khama in

Serowe. In celebration of our 50th anniversary of independence in 2016, a special edition of the New Testament in English was prepared with our national flag on the cover. This included interesting historical information and a short gospel message. Many government officials throughout the country received a personal copy. Two gospel tracts were written for the occasion: one telling the story of the three chiefs who went to see Queen Victoria in 1895 and seek British protection, and the other linking up with our national anthem which declares that our country is a gift from God.

50th Anniversary
New Testament

Gifts of Bible commentaries and other teaching books in English (from John Ritchie, Precious Seed, and Scripture Teaching Library) have been gratefully received from overseas and passed on to those who can make the best use of them. Our Setswana books are aimed at providing basic Bible knowledge to men and women or young folk who may not have had the benefit of higher education. Material of this nature in their own language is scarce, and short introductory guides to the Old and the New Testament are tailored to meet this need. Shorter and simpler English materials written by T. Ernest Wilson and Bert Cargill have proved to be suitable for translation.

A Setswana Bible dictionary (*Thanodi ya Baebele*) took ten years to complete. Our Setswana Bible is based on the English Revised Version. This meant that an English Bible dictionary could not be directly translated into Setswana – the word usage was often different. Every reference for any particular word had to be checked, verse by verse. Special sections were devoted to Christ – His names, words and parables, acts and miracles. Each of the 66 books in the Bible was introduced. Other special sections covered assembly truth and prophecy. The dictionary is now in its second edition.

Setswana Tracts and Books

Modern Trends

Despite higher levels of literacy, the young men and women of today do not seem to have as much interest in reading books as the former generation. University students are accustomed now to having much of their material online. This affects not only what they read but also how they read. Reading a book with concentration for an extended time is becoming less common. The growing use of computers is filtering through to secondary and primary levels of education. The Botswana government plans to set up hubs or terminals throughout the country, even in remote areas, so that local residents can access the internet, receiving the latest information. The hope is that this will facilitate interaction with government departments and people will be able to conduct vital business such as applying for licences and permits without travelling physically to the capital.

Technology is neutral: it can be used for the common good or the common ill. The new era of information technology has meant that the widespread availability of mobile phones and access to social media are having a profound effect on society. The process of transmitting and receiving information is almost instantaneous, but it can also be superficial, rash, and harmful. We are all affected by it. Someone misplaces their Bible and with a casual shrug of the shoulders they say, 'Oh well, it will turn up sometime.' Should they lose their mobile phone, they are suddenly in a state of acute agitation and despair, 'I must find it now!' And if we grow accustomed to arguments presented as tweets, we may find it difficult to concentrate on listening to a Bible teacher patiently presenting an important topic in depth for even 30 minutes.

A glance at church history might help us retain a sense of balance. It would remind us that until the invention and introduction of the printing press in the 15th century (by Johannes Gutenberg in Germany and William Caxton in England), access to reading material was the exclusive preserve of the rich and educated elite. Suddenly, literature including the Bible was made available to a much wider audience. There were prophets of doom back then who lamented the introduction of the new-fangled technology. The common man would now have access to learning, reading his Bible for himself, and forming his own opinions. Nothing good would come of it, was what some believed. History would indicate otherwise. The dissemination of Bible truth not only paved the way for the Reformation of the 16th century, but it also has brought about many a personal and national spiritual revival since then. "The entrance of thy words giveth light" (Psalm 119.130).

During the recent global pandemic, technology has been made use of in ways that promote God's interests in the world. Apart from online occasions for the proclamation of the gospel and for Bible teaching, many gospel tracts and messages have also been posted online. When such efforts are made sincerely and prayerfully, God can bless. At the time of writing, we are all longing for a return to normality as we used to know it. Perhaps it will never come, but rather Christ will soon come to the air and call His people home. Maranatha!

Chapter 17

MEDICAL WORK

The Great Physician

Why did the Lord Jesus Christ spend time healing sick people? Did this not divert Him from His true mission of seeking and saving lost souls? While we may rightly be concerned that there is a danger of sidelining spiritual needs by focussing on social needs such as sickness, poverty, and hunger, there is also a danger of ignoring the truth of the Bible. James, the Lord's half-brother, warned against a profession of faith that overlooks obvious physical need; he indicated that such faith is profitless and dead (James 2.14-17).

The Scriptures show that Christ's healing ministry was a fulfilment of messianic prophecy. According to Dr Luke, Christ stood up in the synagogue in Nazareth and read these words (a quotation from the Septuagint version of Isaiah 61.1-2): "The Spirit of the Lord is upon me, because he hath anointed me to preach the gospel to the poor; he hath sent me to heal the brokenhearted, to preach deliverance to the captives, and recovering of sight to the blind, to set at liberty them that are bruised, to preach the acceptable year of the Lord" (Luke 4.18-19).

Christ's healing ministry was also a demonstration of His

divine love and power. We frequently read of Him being moved with compassion: "And Jesus went about all the cities and villages, teaching in their synagogues, and preaching the gospel of the kingdom, and healing every sickness and every disease among the people. But when he saw the multitudes, he was moved with compassion on them, because they fainted, and were scattered abroad, as sheep having no shepherd" (Matthew 9.35-36). He was "moved with compassion toward them, and healed their sick" (Matthew 14.14). It would be a similar response when He observed that the multitude following Him were hungry: "I have compassion on the multitude, because they … have nothing to eat" (Matthew 15.32). He took time to feed them.

As Christ was leaving Jericho for the last time, on His way to Jerusalem, two blind men called out to Him for mercy. It would have been no surprise to the Saviour that their request to Him was that their eyes should be opened: "So Jesus had compassion on them, and touched their eyes: and immediately their eyes received sight, and they followed him" (Matthew 20.34). The last words are significant; they committed themselves completely to Him. His work in them was deeper than physical healing.

Of the thirty-five or so recorded miracles of Christ, the majority were miracles of healing. Despite the extravagant claims of men, there is nothing comparable seen today. All of the Lord's healing miracles related to serious conditions: leprosy, heart failure, blindness, deafness, paralysis, epilepsy etc. It was evident that these conditions were healed immediately and completely.

Botswana has many self-professed 'faith healers'. Also, there are frequent visitors from outside the country who come and organise several evenings in a large venue. The last evening is described as an all-night prayer, deliverance and healing session. In all my years of clinical work in Botswana, seeing thousands of sick people, I did not see a single patient return and claim they had been completely healed at one of these services. If one of my familiar wheelchair-bound patients had bounded through the door of the clinic, I would not have been able to deny the wonder of it all. It never happened, not even once.

The Nursing Team

Caring for the sick is demanding in terms of time and energy. In a developing country, or in any country for that matter, one can easily become overwhelmed and swamped by the pressure of curative medicine. When people are ill, they require 24-hour care. A doctor who has operated on a patient who subsequently develops post-operative bleeding, cannot morally or legally refuse to attend them with the excuse, 'I am sorry, I have to go now to the prayer meeting at my local church. I will come later.'

Coming later could be too late. This is the challenge that medical missionaries face. Each individual resolves it in his or her own way, as before the Lord. One cannot legislate for another.

In Botswana, we have been privileged to be able to present the terms under which we wished to operate. The government officials welcomed whatever contribution we could make. They also appreciated our willingness to offer our services freely, without expecting payment. This meant that Jim and Irene could run mobile bush clinics several days a week in the villages surrounding Serowe. For two years Hazel and I enjoyed sharing in this work. Much was learnt through the close contact with patients that clinical work demands.

Medicine in 'the bush'

In the village clinics, we functioned as 'jack of all trades and master of none'. At the primary health care level, we were confronted with all sorts of conditions, minor and major. However, in addition to these duties, I was asked to help with difficult obstetric cases in the local hospital in Serowe. This was a welcome link to my former medical speciality. At that time, there was an experienced team of Dutch doctors based in Sekgoma Hospital. When the phone rang and they needed help, one knew it was a difficult case. Sadly, some patients delayed seeking help until it was too late: the baby was already dead in the womb and the priority was to save the life of the mother. In our more normal duties, Irene and Hazel were kept busy as qualified midwives. Years later, it was always a pleasant surprise to come across infants who bore their names.

When Jim and Irene had to stay overnight in village clinics, they would use the occasion to proclaim the gospel in the evening. After we moved to Gaborone in 1984, the situation was somewhat different: the day's work in the government clinics routinely began with a prayer and the singing of a well-known hymn involving both staff and waiting patients. When invited to participate, we had an opportunity to add a reading of Scripture and remark upon it.

In Gaborone, Hazel would come to have many opportunities through vaccination clinics and later through district midwifery to show patients the love of Christ and pass on gospel literature when she did post-natal visits. She elected to visit new mothers in the area of our first Gospel Hall. These contacts were valuable, and we still are approached by patients we have long forgotten but who will never forget the kindness shown to them. MmaWisi was a lady who lost her newborn baby. She was so impressed with the care and concern shown to her by the believers that she began to attend cottage meetings in our own home in Tlokweng village. This led to her trusting Christ and she has continued to prove the reality of life-changing salvation.

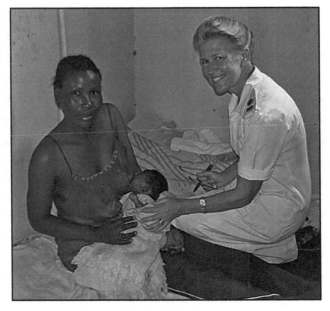

District Midwifery

Health Challenges

Visitors are surprised that there was no statutory requirement for vaccination before travelling to Botswana, at least in pre-Coronavirus days. In general, the dry climate makes Botswana one of the healthier options for those wishing to visit Africa. However, we have always recommended that visitors take malarial prophylaxis. During our rainy season, this serious condition still claims lives. A high index of suspicion is the key to preventing fatalities. Tourists can return home from a malarial area, feel unwell with headache, fever and chills, but delay seeking medical help and quickly succumb to cerebral malaria.

Nearly every year, there are other tourists who come to view our fascinating wildlife but show little respect for the animals in their natural habitat. Foolish young men may regard it as a hilarious sport to charge a wild animal in a sturdy 4x4 vehicle, but some have discovered too late that the lion, buffalo, hippo, or elephant was much wiser than they were, and their vehicle was not as robust as they thought. There are fatalities nearly every year. Snakebites and scorpion stings are not uncommon, and these can be deadly as well. It is not advisable to wander about in the bush at night without a good torch and a heightened level of vigilance. In the morning, it is a wise precaution to check one's footwear before putting them on.

Malnutrition has been less prevalent in Botswana than in other African countries of the region. Even a poorer family might own or have access to a few cattle providing the children with a supply of milk. Foreign aid to Botswana was significant after independence: in the clinics we became accustomed to seeing long lines of patients queuing for supplies of cooking oil, meal and other food items bearing the aid logos of countries such as the UK, the USA, Canada, and Norway. Behind the scenes, overseas experts in public health were also advising and assisting the Ministry of Health to develop the primary health care sector.

Vaccination programmes have radically altered the health and mortality rates of infants. This was an important component of our clinical practice. Irene and Hazel vaccinated thousands of infants against diseases such as diphtheria, whooping cough, and measles. Apart from these childhood illnesses, the major public health issues were TB, then the HIV/AIDS epidemic, followed more recently by the Covid-19 pandemic.

In our own limited experience, we faced disease profiles that we had never seen before and did not fully understand. The year of Sid Halsband's severe neurological illness was a year characterised by a debilitating flu-like illness that took months to resolve and affected many people in Botswana including ourselves. In that same year, the lady who helps in our home gave birth to a baby girl suffering from spina bifida and hydrocephalus. After several months of treatment, the little one died. A Zambian couple in fellowship gave birth to twin girls with severe mental and physical handicap. One died in infancy; the other lived for many years but could never walk, talk or enjoy any semblance of normal life. Her parents loved her and faithfully cared for her until the end. In the same year, our sister Agnes's young son developed a strange meningitis-like illness, the cause of which was never identified. Sometime later, Hazel, after another flu-like illness, developed complications with an ascending paralysis which affected mainly her lower limbs but also her hands and arms. This serious condition has relapsed several times. Each time, after hospitalisation, she has had to learn to walk again. The Lord has given grace to all of these dear believers to cope with these many difficulties.

In 1975, the Ministry of Health established the National Tuberculosis Programme. The focus was on managing the high prevalence of TB, and it seemed that progress was being made until 1985 when Botswana registered its first case of HIV infection. For some time, we had been puzzled by unusual presentations of disease among young people. Instead of them presenting with chickenpox, due to the herpes zoster virus, they were presenting with shingles, the form of the disease that usually affects older people. Others came to the clinic with Bell's palsy, a one-sided facial weakness. We soon came to appreciate that these were just two of the strange effects of inflammation in young patients who were HIV positive. One of the saddest but common occurrences was to have a young woman enter the clinic with a small baby in her arms. The baby was clearly unwell, but the mother too was showing signs of disease. One knew that soon there might be two funerals. Families were decimated with many children left as orphans.

New Opportunities

At the same time, there were opportunities to proclaim the good news of the gospel. World Aids Day would often be organised with us being invited to address large gatherings of people and it was a good opportunity to read from the Bible and apply its truth. One day in a clinic, a local chief who had just tested positive for HIV said to me, 'You Christians are the ones who have the answer.'

Dr Kgosi Mompati became a leader in the field of HIV/AIDS treatment and management. He sought to maintain Christian principles throughout. His medical career has taken several unusual turns. After completing higher training in South Africa and UK, the family settled in Francistown in 1988 and Kgosi worked as a consultant physician in the busy and overcrowded government hospital.

The next year he was asked to accompany President Masire to Washington, USA, as the president's usual attending physician was away on a visit to Canada. The initial meeting at State House was daunting and Kgosi was apprehensive about his heavy responsibilities. However, the state visit to the USA meant that Kgosi was often in the company of the president and he found him to be warm and friendly. They stayed in a luxury hotel and on Sunday morning the president and a number of his aides attended an Episcopal church in Washington. In the evening the

President asked Kgosi where he had worshipped that day and he told him of the local assembly of Christians he had been able to visit that same morning.

On their return to Botswana, Kgosi was formally appointed as the president's personal physician. Other international trips followed all over the world. His appointment also meant a transfer to Gaborone, but it was not possible for Dorcas and the family to move with him. This was the main reason Kgosi eventually resigned from the civil service and entered private practice, along with his wife, in Francistown. Just before leaving his position, he spent a weekend in his home village of Serowe. After he preached the gospel, a young man was saved. Kgosi was encouraged that he was making the right decision. Several job offers came to him from the mining company in Selebi-Phikwe and the colliery near Palapye, but he remained in Francistown to be with his family and to assist in the assembly work there.

The AIDS Epidemic

The epidemic spread like wildfire in Botswana and for many years dominated the minds and practice of health personnel. We registered one of the highest prevalence rates in the world. The TB rates also soared again because those with compromised immunity due to HIV were commonly co-infected with TB. With Botswana's limited financial and logistical resources, it was inevitable that the care of other conditions was sidelined to a degree.

We spent our days attending funerals, while the evenings preceding the funeral were taken up with 'prayers'. The mortuaries and cemeteries could not cope. We recall one Friday afternoon waiting outside one of the many funeral parlours to collect the body of someone we knew. We were given a slip of paper indicating that we were number 40 on their list that day. The customary day for funerals was Saturday, but this had to be extended to include other days of the week because the graveyards were inundated at the weekends. Multiple graves were dug with only narrow strips of land in between. Three or four funeral services might be conducted at one time in close proximity, causing inevitable confusion. Now and again there would be an appeal at the graveside for all of the adjacent funeral services to stop singing different hymns at the same time, in favour of one well-known hymn to be sung by us all.

It affected our assembly life as a local group of believers. Our normal schedule of meetings would often be disrupted because of funeral responsibilities. There were also significant challenges for meetings such as the Lord's Supper. Many families lost their breadwinners and suffered deprivation as a result.

Dr Mompati maintained a busy schedule throughout those years, not only initiating new HIV/AIDS treatment regimens locally but also attending international conferences. At times he faced opposition. When he advocated monogamy and faithfulness in marriage as one of the most effective preventive measures, his critics fired back that he must not know his Bible for Abraham and many others in the Bible had more than one wife. He formulated the AB of prevention which became a national slogan: 'Abstain, Be faithful.' (Others added the next letter, C.) The combination therapies he initiated were successful in allowing patients to extend their lifespan. Many of them continue in general good health after more than 20 years on treatment. The Botswana government would become one of the first in Africa to offer treatment to all patients, despite the great expense of this undertaking. In 2002 it began using the treatment regimen that Kgosi had introduced.

A private hospital, Riverside Hospital, was built in Francistown under Kgosi's direction. In more recent years, kidney dialysis facilities have been established both in Francistown and Palapye. Patients with renal failure no longer need to travel to South Africa as they once did for treatment. Gospel tracts have always been made freely available at these health facilities and several people have trusted Christ and are now in assembly fellowship through these contacts.

President Masisi Opening the Renal Dialysis Unit

Our son, Andrew, after completing university studies in cancer research in Belfast, was offered a post-doctoral research fellowship with Harvard University. While being required to work for some months in Boston, USA, most of his three-year tenure was spent working locally as part of the Mochudi Prevention Project, an ongoing AIDS research initiative in Botswana. His fluency in Setswana meant that he was often called upon to liaise with local chiefs and administrators in promoting disease prevention and organising the protocols. He also was involved in the ongoing education programme of the Cancer Association of Botswana.

The Coronavirus Pandemic

This book is being written during the Covid-19 pandemic. All over the world, people have had to comply with government regulations that have greatly limited their normal way of life. In Botswana, we remain grateful for the leadership of our nation and the medical and nursing staff who have laboured to keep us safe. In comparison to our neighbouring countries, especially South Africa, we have been preserved in large measure so far. We realise that the pandemic is not over yet and the situation can deteriorate rapidly. Several lockdowns and curfews have all been introduced since the pandemic began.

At present, we can meet as a local church twice a week with a limit on our numbers. We are obliged to register, sanitise, check the temperature of all attendees, and wear masks. We must practise social distancing and we do not sing during the services. In general, the population has been compliant and understanding of these restrictions. We have been spared the complaints and refusals that have so afflicted some other countries.

The major challenges remain of encouraging older and more isolated saints who cannot meet regularly with us. Our large Sunday School work and regular gospel work have been severely disrupted. We miss the contact with the hundreds of children we saw each week. By various other means including online meetings, we have sought to continue providing Bible teaching for the assembly members. New gospel tracts and pocket calendars have been produced and distributed. The open-air preaching continues by remaining in the vehicle and using a loudspeaker. People often listen from their own homes. We have been encouraged to know of those we have long prayed for who have trusted Christ recently. God is still mighty to save!

Several assembly members have tested positive for Coronavirus, so we felt it wise on these occasions to discontinue the meetings in the hall for two weeks to allow the situation to clarify. Even as I write today, we have just heard of the passing of an elderly man from Francistown, the first assembly believer we know of who has died here from a Covid-19 infection. Rre Munyadzwe will be remembered as a quiet and gracious Christian gentleman.

We do not know what the months ahead will bring us. But for now, we remain thankful, trusting in the Lord who has promised to be with us through all the different experiences of life.

Chapter 18

CHILDREN'S WORK

The Lord Jesus Christ had a deep love and care for little children.[5] When they came to Him, He took each of them up in His arms and blessed them. The disciples had a different mindset; they would have chased the children away. Their hearts were out of tune with the heart of their Master. They regarded the children as something of a nuisance or distraction and not that important. Perhaps they thought that giving time to little ones was beneath them; the children's work could be conveniently left to the next batch of young novice recruits. Such attitudes still prevail.

The Lord Jesus did not spare His disciples. He was sorely displeased and immediately corrected their glaring error, saying to them, "Suffer the little children to come unto me, and forbid them not: for of such is the kingdom of God … Whosoever shall not receive the kingdom of God as a little child, he shall not enter therein" (Mark 10.14-15). The Saviour recognised the importance of the children, not only for their own sake but also for what they represented; a simple, unquestioning faith. That was the kind of faith He valued most in His kingdom.

In our own experience of serving the Lord in Botswana, we have seen the importance of children's work. It is not that we regard ourselves as specialists in this age group – the gospel is for everyone and no one should be neglected – but the interest that young children have shown and continue to show in coming to hear the Word of God has developed into a large and fruitful work.

Enthusiasm!

The Value of Children's Work

Several factors combine to make children's work in Botswana a vital area of service. Over half of the population is under 20 years of age. We enjoy a high literacy rate among the young. While one might still see an elderly person sign their pension book in the Post Office by making a thumbprint, most children can read and write; they love to receive any form of gospel literature. Tracts and gospel booklets have been produced especially for young ones. Over the years, dozens of children have come to faith in Christ. Even today, 50 years after the commencement of the work, most of the men and women in assembly fellowship will relate that it was as a child that they first heard the gospel and were saved.

A boy or girl trusting Christ could be likened to a new candle that, God willing, can burn over a whole lifetime for His glory. Not only is a soul saved but also a life is saved. By His grace, that life will be preserved from the effects of sin, both physical and spiritual. An adult has already lost years that could have been lived for Christ. The renowned preacher, D. L. Moody, appreciated the value of a childhood conversion and a whole life, not just part of it, devoted to the service of Christ. One evening he returned from preaching and reported that he had just witnessed 'two and a half conversions'. When his host enquired, 'Two adults and a child?' Moody replied, 'Oh no, two children and an adult.'

Another valuable result of children's work is that it opens up to us the homes and hearts of the parents. On many occasions, a child has been saved and then has begun to bring his or her mother to the gospel meeting. The mother has been saved and one finds a sudden and wonderful change – a household has now become a Christian home.

If children are valuable, they are also vulnerable. We are often deeply shocked these days with news headlines from all around the world telling of the evil abuse and exploitation of little children. Maybe such a thing has always been happening, but it does seem more prevalent and shameless now. It is only by the mercy of God that small children can be preserved. The number of orphans and street children increases year by year.

We take heart, however, when we read the story of Samuel. Gross evil was all around, even in the environs of the tabernacle. Eli's sons were the worst role models one could ever find. Yet the Scriptures show time and again that the boy was preserved and made progress in the things of God. (See 1 Samuel 2.11-12; 17-18; 21-22; 25-26). He went on to make a mark for God in his day.

A Sunday School teacher can be a stabilising and sanctifying influence on young children. Some of them grow up in difficult household environments (often with a single parent, usually a mother) where both love and discipline are lacking at times; but every week they know that they have a teacher who will welcome them with a smile. Constant care is shown to them and a consistent standard lived before them so that the child, while learning the truth of the Word of God, also sees and understands how Christians act.

These children never forget you because you have become, in many ways, a special friend to them. We are frequently greeted by name by young men and women in the street. When we struggle to put names to the faces they quickly remind us that they once attended Sunday School. In our embarrassment at not recognising them, we used to be rather vague and general in our reply. That was until a few quick-witted ones started asking, 'You do know who I am, don't you?' This led to our frequent confession: 'Sorry, we can't remember. It was 30 years ago, and you have grown and changed a lot since we first knew you.'

The Growth of the Work

In Serowe, the work of the Sunday School in tandem with the opportunities in schools meant that many children were familiar with RraJudi and MmaJudi and the location of the Ntlo ya Efangele. Jim and Irene began to train additional teachers as the Sunday School grew. There was a rapid expansion in the 90s so that at one time almost 1,000 children were attending each week. There was much blessing in salvation among the young and several large families saw nearly all of their members saved. A Bible Class was aimed at meeting the needs of the new believers and helping them grow in the knowledge of the Word.

Similarly, large numbers of children have attended Sunday School in all of the other assembly locations in Botswana. There is an ebb and flow in terms of attendance, and yet we remain thankful for the open door of acceptance with the boys and girls who come every week. In Gaborone and the surrounding villages of Mochudi, Rasesa, Kopong and Tlokweng, we have been able to hold over 12 weekly classes. Many hundreds of children attend. Several believers are involved, depending on when they can be free. On a number of weekdays, classes are held concurrently in different venues. Some of these Sunday Schools have commenced as a result of invitations from local people to help their children; they have made their home yards available to us. Visiting the children in their home villages also does away with the need to transport them. At the weekends, local believers from the assembly bear the main responsibility for teaching the Sunday Schools in the two Gospel Halls at Broadhurst and Gaborone West.

In the villages, it is a delight to arrive to such a warm welcome: we often sound the horn as we approach and there, under a large tree, dozens of children are already waiting. They begin to jump up and down excitedly, from foot to foot, singing and calling out their teacher's name. Who would not enjoy such a keen and appreciative audience? When a new wave of children starts attending, they quickly learn what is expected of them. Those under a year old are a challenge at times – they may fall asleep or begin crying if they see someone else getting a sweet for answering a question. They do not understand why they are missing out. We are careful now to ensure that every child gets at least one sweet for attending.

Sometimes we are asked, 'How do you cope with discipline when there are so many coming?' There are few problems in this regard. The children are coming voluntarily, and they value the time spent with their Sunday School teacher. They sit up, sing up (in beautiful natural harmony), and listen up. In our experience, particularly in the village Sunday Schools, one person can sit under a tree with over 100 children at his or her feet and have a fully engaged and attentive audience. One notable exception was a mischievous little boy known to everyone as 'Tomtom'. Rather than sit under the tree, he preferred to climb the tree and shout down from his perch above, entertaining everyone below with his funny remarks. Since he has grown up and left the Sunday School, he is rather missed. It has also been encouraging from time to time when mothers also join us. The age range can then extend from six months to fifty!

The annual prize-givings have always been a highlight of the year and the parents are as keen to attend as the children. The gospel is always presented on such occasions. Many of the boys and girls come from poor homes so they are delighted to receive good prizes for attendance and verse recitation: a first prize might include a Bible, some items of clothing, stationery, toiletries, and maybe a small toy. We used to receive regularly mailed parcels from assemblies and individuals overseas. The Women's Missionary Fellowship was also a faithful contributor, sending out items including many that were handmade. These parcels were packed with suitable materials for making up hundreds of prizes. We would pick them up at the local post office and often look wide-eyed at the dozens of postage stamps adhering to them.

Great expense, as well as great effort, were involved in making up and sending these parcels. Our hearts were often touched to think of the sacrificial giving such work entailed.

In more recent years, a container has been shipped annually from Northern Ireland in connection with the Kells assembly and believers of Cambridge Avenue assembly in Ballymena. This has involved teamwork and much labour. Their contribution has been invaluable, and they remain a convenient channel for individuals and assemblies wanting to send supplies to us here. Once again, we are indebted to all those from overseas who have been exercised to share in this work. They have done so faithfully, efficiently, and generously. We are encouraged to know that the Lord will reward them fully.

The Joy of Prize Day

Locally, a dedicated group of sisters from the Gaborone assembly begins meeting weekly from January onwards. They continue working throughout the year, making up 1,500 prizes for the end of the year. It is a major logistical challenge to organise, sort, select, bag, label, and store all of these items in advance. These ladies have also been able to assist various believers in more isolated areas with prizes for their children too. In other assemblies, the sisters are similarly engaged.

Work in Schools

As mentioned previously, doors have opened in remarkable ways in Serowe, Palapye and elsewhere to teach the Scriptures in state schools and even in several private schools. The trend in curriculum development is now towards a multi-faith approach with the emphasis shifting to teaching moral education and ethics rather than instruction in Bible knowledge. And yet, there is considerable leeway in individual cases for the Bible still to be taught without compromise. A good and positive relationship with the headteacher has been vital in maintaining an open door.

Bible Distribution in Schools

For many years Hazel had an invitation to make weekly visits to a playschool in Gaborone. Our two children had attended there when they were small. Despite being the only Europeans there, they fitted in and were well received. Their fluency in Setswana made the difference. One might think that small children are limited in their capacity to learn, but Hazel was often amazed at how much they retained and understood.

At the end of every year, there was an official-looking graduation ceremony for the children who would soon be leaving. All the vital elements were included – gowns, mortarboards, and even diplomas for the four and five-year-old 'scholars'. The patroness of the playschool then was the President's wife, Lady Masire. She would arrive early, roll up her sleeves, and join the staff in arranging chairs. Often her husband, the President, attended, and they and their special guests would listen to the children singing choruses and repeating the gospel verses they had learned, and watch them act out a Bible story. Occasionally there was an invitation for us to open the Scriptures and deliver a brief message. We recall how that every year, President Masire would take our fair-haired little daughter, Sethunya, up in his arms and give her a kiss. Everybody seemed to know Sethunya!

All of us who have served the Lord in Botswana have shared the desire to see our own children come to faith in Christ. Many have done so, and often their testimony as young believers has spoken to their friends and others. At the local secondary school, our daughter was on the netball team, but she declined to play sport on Sunday. Unknown to us at the time, she was sent to the headmaster who expressed his disappointment, telling her that she was letting the school down. She replied, 'Sir, may I ask a question?' The headmaster said that she could. 'Well, sir, why is it that children of other faiths are exempt from sports when they have to attend prayers or fast, but when I as a Christian wish to attend my church, I am criticised?' The headmaster paused and then replied, 'Yes, Heather, that is true. You've got a point there.' The outcome was that Heather was allowed to miss the matches on Sundays, provided she could organise someone to take her place.

The Challenges

No country stands still and there are changes in Botswana affecting the attitudes and values of young ones. Widespread access to television and the internet means that children are becoming more sophisticated in a worldly sense. However, we continue to be thankful for the numbers who still come each week to sing a few choruses, learn verses from the Word of God, and listen to a simple lesson with a gospel application.

School life has become more demanding and competitive. No longer does primary or secondary school work end around midday. There are now many other activities that children must attend, often in the afternoons but also on weekends. There is one term when sports are prominent and another term when traditional dancing and singing keep the children busy. One can find that a mid-week or Saturday 'Sunday School' suddenly becomes smaller because so many of the boys and girls are missing. Some of them have been known to slip away early from school activities to make it in time for Sunday School.

The greatest need of all is a spiritual one, not a practical one. How can we make the best use of the opportunities and the many open doors we enjoy at present? How can we spend and be spent for these precious young lives to make sure that this generation of boys and girls hears the good news of the Saviour and His love?

Christ Loved "The Little Children"

The Blessings

Over the years we have had the joy of seeing many boys and girls saved, most of them as first-generation believers. What gives us even more joy is to see them going on well and growing in the things of God. Eventually, they have been baptised and added to the local assembly of believers. In the goodness of the Lord, they find a suitable partner, marry, and have a family of their own. Whereas in early years, there were only first-generation believers, now we are seeing a new generation who have the privilege of being brought up in a Christian home.

We thank the Lord for the godly young couples who presently grace the local assemblies. We are grateful too for brethren who have developed into 'Timothys' and true shepherds of the flock.

For many, it all started in a Sunday School. Will the subsequent generations have the same commitment as their parents? We cannot tell. But what we are sure of is this: our Lord made no mistake when He welcomed the little ones into His arms. Heaven will be full of those who, as children, came to know the Holy Scriptures which made them "wise unto salvation through faith which is in Christ Jesus" (2 Timothy 3.15).

She was only a little girl when she began attending the Sunday School. She lived at the end of the street; her family came from Uganda. She was also one of the most intelligent children in my wife's class, able to learn chapter after chapter of Scripture. One day, Hazel casually remarked to her: 'I really don't know what passage I can give you to learn next, Caroline. Maybe, Psalm 119?' The reply came back, 'Alright, I'll learn it.' Despite her not knowing that it was the longest chapter in the Bible – 176 verses – learn it she did. When she came to recite it, she did so without making one mistake.

Her family moved away to Swaziland, but Hazel kept in touch with her. One night, the young woman came on the phone in great distress. She had been reading her Bible, in the book of Revelation. She confessed that she could not understand it all, but she could see that judgment was coming and she was not ready. Slowly and patiently she was told of how she could be saved and be sure that she was ready. That night, talking over the phone, Caroline was saved.

This is only one of the amazing stories of grace we have been privileged to witness among the young. There are many others that we and our colleagues could tell.

Chapter 19

PRISON WORK

The Bible records numerous incidents that occurred in prison. It is a theme that can be traced from Genesis to Revelation. Many of God's choicest servants have spent long periods in prison where they have suffered unjustly because of their faithfulness to God. And yet what wonderful experiences they had there – God was with them! At times, they received special revelations from Himself. We recall men like Joseph and Jeremiah in the Old Testament, and Peter and Paul in the New Testament. Paul's 'prison Epistles' are masterpieces.

In more recent times we have accounts of similar suffering from the pens of men like the late Geoffrey Bull who was detained for over three years by Chinese communists. His writings are vivid and challenging. For every known detainee there are dozens of others today, virtually unknown, who are similarly imprisoned and suffering for Christ. As they languish in harsh, dehumanising conditions, their earnest prayer must be, 'O Lord, how long?'

The focus of this chapter will be to relate how God is still at work and revealing Himself to men and women in prison. The significant difference in our case is that the people we have visited were imprisoned because of their misdeeds. And yet, God loves them and the power of the gospel of Christ can transform them.

One of the messianic promises spoke of Christ as bringing "liberty to the captives" (Isaiah 61.1) and we have had the privilege of witnessing this in a spiritual as well as a physical sense.

Prisons are found in most large towns and villages throughout Botswana. Opportunities have arisen to visit these institutions. Each prison will have at least one official chaplain on the regular staff; he chooses and invites others to come to preach and teach from the Bible, usually every week. Ideally, visits should be regular but at times opportunities have arisen to make occasional visits to other more distant prisons.

A Prison Officer Converted

In Serowe, Jim Legge visited both the men's and women's prisons for many years. Those of us who spent time in Serowe for language study had the privilege of accompanying Jim. Numbers varied – at times there could be a very large audience – but perfect liberty was always granted to proclaim the gospel in its fulness. Prisoners in Botswana like to sing and there would usually be a rendition of several choruses that they knew. When it was time to listen to the Word of God, they were reverent and attentive. Gospel literature, tracts and booklets, were widely distributed among the inmates. Those who were keen to study could receive Setswana Bible courses. Jim would review the written answers the prisoners gave to the questions in the lessons; often these provided insight into a prisoner's understanding of biblical truths. There were times too when the prison officers requested their own Bible study and Jim was only too willing to oblige.

This weekly routine continued for many years in Serowe. One of the outstanding results was the salvation of a lady prison officer we know as MmaTumelo (the mother of Tumelo). Her home village was Oodi, not far from Gaborone, but as is the custom in government service, she was posted to various places throughout the country. Not only did she find salvation in the prison in Serowe after hearing Jim preach, but also she was baptised there. After being transferred to Gaborone she was received into assembly fellowship and has been a most faithful believer for many years. She has long retired from the prison service.

MmaTumelo

We recall the tragedy she faced when the police came to her home in the village of Oodi and reported that the body of her only son, Tumelo, had been found beside a small river in the bush and he had been dead for several days. When MmaTumelo was called to the mortuary in Gaborone to identify the body, she was only able to do so by feeling an old scar on the back of his scalp. The funeral was expedited so that he was buried by moonlight in his home village. The exact cause of death was never established. Like so many of our older believers, she bravely faced up to the loss and continued to trust in the Lord. She was left with a daughter.

A Prisoner Converted

After we moved to Gaborone, we received permission to visit the prison complex. At one time we were visiting three times a week – the Boy's Prison, the Women's Prison, and the high-security prison. The ease of our work depended much on the cooperation of the prison staff and the resident chaplain.

The Boys' Prison was a misnomer. I rarely saw anyone that could be described as a boy. They all looked like adult men and I came to learn, although I never asked, that many of them had committed serious crimes. This was not merely a holding area for junior pickpockets and those who had committed petty offences. Attendance at our meetings was voluntary for the prisoners. As in Serowe, month after month, the gospel was proclaimed. At times one wondered what the inmates were thinking and whether or not the gospel meeting was merely a break in the otherwise monotonous routine. Whatever their motivation to attend, we were only too glad to have the opportunity to speak of Christ. Occasionally, a few would wait behind to speak personally and expressed their desire to have a Bible, be saved, and join the church, all within the space of a few weeks. One gained a sense of their sincerity by the regularity of their attendance.

It was not until October of 1985 that one of the inmates, who had been attending for almost two years, professed faith in Christ (see Chapter 7). After Oitlogetse's release, he regularly attended the assembly meetings. He was baptised, received into fellowship, and he began to help with teaching the Sunday School and preaching the gospel. His spiritual growth was an encouragement to us because at that time there were only a few believers. He was always welcome in our home and at our table. Hazel would head to the kitchen to prepare him something tasty; he often referred to her as 'the bachelor's friend'.

One day he came to tell me about a young woman he was interested in. She seemed to be an earnest Christian and he was thinking of proposing marriage to her. We chatted for a time and it became clear that this young woman belonged to a group of people that were known for their clean lifestyle. However, they taught error concerning important aspects of the gospel. I tried to break this to him gently, suggesting that there could be problems ahead. He did not proceed any further in the relationship. Years later, he confessed that the counsel given to him that day was like 'an injection' – painful at the time but ending up doing him good.

MmaTumelo was transferred to Gaborone and she was a useful person to know on the staff of the Women's Prison. I was granted about half an hour there to speak to the women. Once again, attendance was voluntary; some women remained in their cells. When MmaTumelo was on duty, I would be admitted in good time and the meeting would be already organised in terms of seating and attendance. Things ran somewhat less smoothly when she was not there. It was sad on occasions to see women imprisoned with their small infants, but this was preferable to them being separated from their children.

'Saved at Midnight' Gospel Tract

A Cautionary Tale

We were informed of a prisoner who had been transferred from his home village to the high-security wing in Gaborone. He came from a wealthy family but seemed bent on a life of crime. Having heard the gospel, he had professed faith in Christ. After obtaining permission to visit him, it was an unusual experience to go through the large steel gates set in high walls. The other two prisons mentioned had their perimeters secured by barbed-wire fences and gates but were much more open in appearance.

This particular inmate was charming, intelligent, and eloquent. As a perceptive friend commented after we visited him together, 'That young man will either turn out to be the greatest saint or the greatest devil.' This also echoed my own unspoken thoughts. We began to study one of Paul's epistles together. He was able to analyse a chapter and expound it like an expert, as if he had been leading Bible studies all his life. I lent him a copy of *Shadow of the Almighty*, the biography of Jim Elliot, that had so influenced me as a young man. After reading it, he returned it with lots of words and phrases marked and underlined, just where I would have marked it had it been my practice to do so.

Not long before his release, he showed me an advertisement from a local newspaper concerning the sale of commercial factories costing hundreds of thousands of Pula. I wondered to myself, how would he ever manage to obtain so much money? Clearly, his mind was now focused on other things. Despite his fervent promises that when he left prison he would come along to 'our church' and thank the Christians for their prayers and kindness, that never happened. I did manage to visit him after his release but all he could talk about was business. The last I heard of him was that he had returned to criminal activities and was again in prison.

These stories illustrate the realities of this kind of work. We know that the real test of a profession of faith occurs after a prisoner is released. The easiest course of action for them is to slip back into their old way of life and reacquaint themselves with their former associates. In some cases, they have even picked up additional nefarious skills in prison. Reoffending is not uncommon.

A Project to Help

With this in mind, Sid Halsband in Maun sought to help prisoners after their release. One of the inmates at the Boro Prison Farm had become a committed believer and gave help with the prison Bible studies which Sid was conducting there at the time. As the prisoner neared the day of his release, there were concerns about employment in the days ahead. After consultation with the prison authorities, Sid set up what he called the Maun Integration Project (MIP).

MIP was a brick-making business that guaranteed three months of employment to male ex-prisoners. The aim was to further their rehabilitation by helping them reintegrate into society. To encourage the participants, each prisoner was paid weekly according to the number of bricks he had produced. Twice a week they attended services at the local assembly. The bricks were sold locally at a reduced price and all the proceeds went back into the project, to pay wages and restock on materials. Local people were happy to buy these bricks and the project was a good testimony in the neighbourhood.

Over the four years or so of the project, about 50 ex-prisoners were assisted. The first of these, the believer who had been contacted initially in the Boro Prison Farm, became the project manager. He showed drive and commitment and he was a responsible leader. Eventually, he returned to his home village.

Refugees and Immigrants

Brethren in Francistown have had good opportunities in the past to visit the local prisons and preach. Correspondence courses have also been well received. It also helped that one of the female prison officers has been saved in connection with the witness of the local assembly. She remains in fellowship in Francistown. The prison chaplains have also been sympathetic and helpful in organising these visits.

Dukwi Prize-giving

The door also opened for visits to the Dukwi Refugee Camp. This is a large camp accommodating several thousands of people from other African countries who are seeking asylum in Botswana. It is some 80 miles from Francistown on the road to Nata. Over the years Jim Legge, Ian Rees, David and Helen McKillen, and John Bandy were able to visit, preach the gospel and speak to the many children there. Official permission to visit was a vital prerequisite for this outreach, and the Lord opened up the way. Literature was distributed and practical assistance was also given. The Sunday School supplies and other suitable items that came by container were put to good use in alleviating the material needs of the refugees.

Nearer to Francistown, a large centre for illegal immigrants was newly constructed on the outskirts of the city. Through the good offices of one of the chaplains, regular visits were arranged for preaching and teaching the Word. The inmates were keen to listen and learn. As is so common in Botswana, the brethren would sometimes be greeted in the street by former prisoners who remembered their visits to the centre or the prison.

John Bandy relates that, over 10 years ago, he and his wife were driving through the city when they noticed a commotion nearby. Police officers were chasing a man who was trying to escape. The story came to light that the man had murdered a child and was trying to evade arrest. After being imprisoned, he began to attend the Bible studies until one day he announced that he was a changed man and he was now born again. He was also a keen student of the correspondence courses. After some months he was transferred to the Gaborone prison where later he was executed for his crime. Several years afterwards, a young girl started to attend the Sunday School in Francistown. It was noticed that she had the same name as the deceased prisoner. It was his daughter.

We thank God for these many opportunities to reach out to those who find themselves in difficult circumstances, often through their own misdeeds. God's love is big enough to include them and His grace is wide enough to forgive them when they come in repentance and faith to the Saviour of sinners. Indeed, were we not all condemned prisoners, enslaved to a cruel master, until the Lord set us free?

Chapter 20

JOY IN THE MORNING

One of the greatest joys in my life is to sit under a tree in an African village with an open Setswana Bible in my hand. It matters not whether the audience is a single individual or a large crowd of boys and girls, but to be able to speak of a God who loves all and a Saviour who died for all is a soul-thrilling occupation. There is nothing quite like it.

On the wider front, those of us serving the Lord in Botswana have rejoiced in the blessing of God as He has opened doors for the gospel, saved souls, planted assemblies, and raised up godly men to care for them. We would all agree, "Hitherto hath the Lord helped us" (1 Samuel 7.12).

The ebb and flow of missionary work has been alluded to already. Much of it is made up of daily routine with nothing outwardly spectacular. Times of blessing are interspersed with periods of apparent leanness. And yet, we would not be anywhere else. We simply responded to God's call. Even in times of loneliness and testing, our Lord is always with us. He has promised never to leave us nor forsake us (Hebrews 13.5).

God has been faithful, and even as we have come to know Him in a deeper way and sought a closer walk with Him, we have learnt more of our own weakness and failings. He is ever gracious and gentle with us slow learners, even as we stumble along. We cannot take credit for anything. The work is His, the blessing is His, and without the Lord, we can do nothing (John 15.5).

The Joy of Opportunities

We remain thankful for the peace and stability of Botswana. We cannot take these blessings for granted because as we know, in such uncertain times, political upheavals can occur overnight anywhere in the world. No country is immune. We continue to pray for our national leaders and all those in authority, "that we may lead a quiet and peaceable life in all godliness and honesty" (1 Timothy 2.2).

The liberty we enjoy in our country is another cause for thanksgiving. We have freedom of movement and freedom of speech. Over the years, the gospel has been proclaimed, both publicly and privately, in a wide variety of places in the cities, towns, and villages of our land, as described in the previous chapters.

We hope that gospel zeal will be maintained in days to come. The increasing busyness of life in Botswana means that it requires an unwavering commitment to keep first things first. Priorities can sometimes be lost sight of, to the detriment of the Lord's work. Materialism and worldliness are constant dangers that threaten to cloud our vision.

The Joy of Blessing in Salvation

The story told out in Acts 8, concerning the meeting of Philip the evangelist and the Ethiopian eunuch, has a special appeal to all of us who serve the Lord in a desert land in Africa. This man who had been seeking after God and reading the Scriptures, was introduced by Philip to the Saviour who suffered and died for sinners. After trusting Christ and being baptised, "he went on his way rejoicing" (Acts 8.39).

Many lives have been transformed by the power of the gospel of Christ. Men and women, boys and girls, who have been burdened and troubled by their sins, have found forgiveness and been reconciled to God. The new life of Christ within them has been evidenced by a change in both their motivation and lifestyle.

Mention has already been made of the dozens of children who have been saved over the years. Our prayer is that they might be preserved. Our desire has always been that those who have been saved should continue well on the Christian pathway and join with us in assembly testimony. Sadly, not all go on well. We are all the more thankful for those who have made steady progress and are living lives that honour God. Many have become an asset to a local assembly and are proving to be a rich blessing to others. They give us hope for tomorrow.

There have been memorable periods of reaping when many souls have been saved. More commonly, there have been months and even years of sowing the gospel seed without visible results. Faith, hope and patience are required to keep going. God has promised that His Word will not return to Him void, but it will accomplish His purposes and prosper in His own time (Isaiah 55.11).

The Joy of Assembly Fellowship

While we have nothing to boast of in terms of numbers, we treasure the fact that assemblies of believers have been established in different parts of Botswana. We pray that they will grow spiritually and numerically. We often use the picture of a fire to illustrate the importance of assembly fellowship. A log removed from the fire and set to the side will quickly lose its warmth and light. So too will a believer who neglects meeting regularly with other believers.

In our individual lives, it is a major step forward when we begin to think less of ourselves and have more concern for others. The love of Christ has been poured into us to flow out of us. When an assembly of Christians abounds in that love, everyone benefits. Each believer has a particular need: it may be spiritual, but it could also be practical or even emotional. We should rise to the occasion and help to carry one another's burdens. We too have been richly blessed when in times of difficulty and ill health, our fellow believers have been quick to draw near and support us through the crisis.

The six assemblies in Botswana have had many years of harmony and unity in the work of the Lord. Unity is fragile and can be easily disturbed. The devil would take delight if we gave him an opportunity to divide us. At times, he has sought to weaken us from within, using moral failure to mar the testimony. At other times, he has tried to disturb the work by stirring up doctrinal differences and encouraging a rebellious spirit. The Bible would remind us that these have been his methods down through the centuries.

It sobers us to recall that of the many assemblies the apostle Paul saw planted in the Roman province of Asia Minor and elsewhere, little remains today, at least in a geographical sense. While it is wise to be burdened as the future of any work of God, and plan for continuity, it is to be balanced by the realisation that it is God's work. Different places have experienced seasons of special blessing, but changes do come, and not all of them are avoidable.

The Joy of Shepherding

God has raised up men who are motivated by His love and empowered by His Spirit. They have taken up the responsibility to care for the flock. In several of the assemblies in Botswana, these are relatively young men who share the burden of guiding and guarding the assembly believers. They have a heavy responsibility, but we are often cheered to hear of their diligence in applying themselves to this work.

Shepherding is learnt on the job, working together and encouraging one another. The maturity and experience of the older brethren are blended with the energy and zeal of the younger generation. It is a happy fusion of complementary strengths and abilities.

The apostle Paul encouraged younger men like Timothy and Titus. He valued their friendship and he wrote to them to strengthen them for the days ahead. This principle of training the upcoming generation has been vital down through the centuries since the Church began. The young Thessalonian church emulated the very things they had seen in the lives of the apostles concerning their manner of life, their preaching, and their ministry of love.

There is no new truth; the same truth is to be passed down to a new generation. However, it never grows stale; it is always fresh and relevant in every age. In this way, the torch of testimony is faithfully passed on and kept burning. May it be so in Botswana.

Joy through Trials

It would remiss of us to give the impression that the work of the Lord in Botswana has been one long and smooth path of progress. We have indicated already that there have been times of pain and sorrow, but God has shown us His gracious hand in blessing time and again. It is His work and we are privileged to share in it. He has also fortified us through His Word and encouraged us to keep going. The Bible reminds us that the pathway to joy is often one of trials and difficulties.

Long ago, a godly man called Nehemiah declared that "the joy of the Lord is your strength" (Nehemiah 8.10). He was speaking to a people who were weeping. It was Dr Luke who recorded that Peter and the apostles were "rejoicing that they were counted worthy to suffer shame for his [Christ's] name" (Acts 5.41). They had just been beaten. When Paul encouraged the Philippian Christians to "Rejoice in the Lord alway: and again I say, Rejoice" (Philippians 4.4), he was writing from prison. These and many other verses show that Christian joy can be experienced, even when the going is hard. It is a joy that does not depend upon the changing winds of external circumstances; it flows from the unchanging spiritual realities within the heart of one whose trust is in God alone.

The Lord Jesus Christ was able to see beyond His pain and suffering to the glorious outcome: "Who for the joy that was set before him endured the cross, despising the shame" (Hebrews 12.2). The apostle Peter wrote of "the sufferings of Christ, and the glory that should follow" (1 Peter 1.11).

The Best is Yet to Come

While many joys can be known even now on earth, the joy of heaven will excel all of these. The darkness of the night will be banished forever by the glory of a celestial dawn. Christ our Lord will see the fruit of the travail of His soul and be satisfied (Isaiah 53.11). And for us, the labours and trials, sorrows and sadness will be over and give way to eternal bliss. Faithful service will be rewarded when they that have sown in tears shall reap in joy (Psalm 126.5).

Much that we cannot see now will be revealed then. Words and deeds we had long forgotten will be brought to light – a brief testimony spoken here, a gospel tract offered there, a spontaneous act of kindness proffered to this one, a helping hand extended to that one, or a brief 'arrow' prayer winged heavenward for another soul in a time of need. All of these, done for His sake, will be shown to have borne fruit and brought eternal blessing to many souls.

It will be a special joy to meet people from Botswana, this desert land, who responded to the gospel. Some we will already know, but others will be a surprise to us. Indeed, heaven will be full of surprises as the fulness of the abundant and glorious harvest is revealed. It will all have been worth it.

We are sure that Samuel Rutherford would allow us to rephrase his lines:

If one soul from Botswana
Meet me at God's right hand,
My heaven will be two heavens
In Immanuel's land.

Ka moso go bo go tle boitumelo

Joy cometh in the morning *(Psalm 30.5)*

ENDNOTES

In several sections of this book, the author has used excerpts of his work from previously published material. (These are marked in the text by numerals in superscript.) Permission to do so is gratefully acknowledged.

[1]Echoes of Service magazine article: *'The Setswana Bible'* (April 1988).

[2]Echoes of Service magazine article: *'Arnot and Khama the Great'* (December 1989).

[3]Echoes of Service magazine article: *'Visiting Kolobeng'* (June 1991).

[4]Scripture Teaching Library book chapter in *'Shepherding the Sheep'* (September 2020).

[5]Truth and Tidings magazine article: *'Little Children'* (October 2009).

Life's Greatest Quest
by Clark Logan

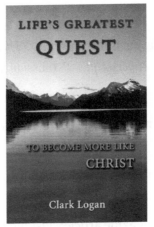

ISBN 9781904064954

Available from:
www.ritchiechristianmedia.co.uk

Christianity in Action
by Clark Logan

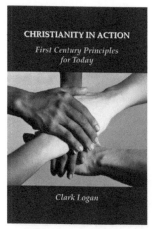

ISBN 9781907731990

Available from:
www.ritchiechristianmedia.co.uk

His Voice in the Morning
by Clark Logan

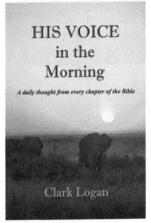

ISBN 9781910513873

Available from:
www.ritchiechristianmedia.co.uk

Cover to Cover
by Clark Logan

ISBN 9781912522392

Available from:
www.ritchiechristianmedia.co.uk

Higher Ground
by Clark Logan

ISBN 9781912522910

Available from:
www.ritchiechristianmedia.co.uk